The Transitory Museum

The Transitory Museum

Emanuele Coccia
Donatien Grau

Translated by Tom Conley

polity

First published in French as *Le musée transitoire* © Editions Klincksieck, 2018

This English edition copyright © Emanuele Coccia and Donantien Grau, 2019

Polity Press
65 Bridge Street
Cambridge CB2 1UR, UK

Polity Press
101 Station Landing
Suite 300
Medford, MA 02155, USA

ISBN-13: 978-1-5095-3304-6
ISBN-13: 978-1-5095-3305-3 (pb)

A catalogue record for this book is available from the British Library.

Typeset in 12.5 on 15 pt Adobe Garamond by
Servis Filmsetting Ltd, Stockport, Cheshire
Printed and bound in Great Britain by Clays Ltd, Elcograf S.p.A.

The publisher has used its best endeavours to ensure that the URLs for external websites referred to in this book are correct and active at the time of going to press. However, the publisher has no responsibility for the websites and can make no guarantee that a site will remain live or that the content is or will remain appropriate.

Every effort has been made to trace all copyright holders, but if any have been overlooked the publisher will be pleased to include any necessary credits in any subsequent reprint or edition.

For further information on Polity, visit our website: politybooks.com

Contents

Preface   In Action   vii

1   Absolute Commerce   1
2   The Eternal and the Ephemeral   38
3   The Far Ends of Fashion   93

Postface   At Calm   127
Notes   131

v

Preface

In Action

It could be anytime in the day. We are walking down a pedestrian street in Milan. Only a few decades ago it was almost dilapidated, deserted; today, well-paved, cutting its way among equally recent high financial towers, it bustles with people. At a corner of an address—number 10—we see blue and green glass panels whose well-traced and separated colors meet and open onto a pathway. Above, we glimpse some tufts of vegetation: even plants have a life here.

Above all, one is in for a surprise; for groups—not isolated individuals, who are there as well, but groups—sneak between two sections that leave a winding path, to enter a completely green garden. Alongside this garden three rooms of a hotel overlook the levels of the courtyard. In the courtyard there's almost no flower, but there is instead greenery that generates a vegetal atmosphere, oxygen. Left and right lie tables and terraces, once you pass this wall of shrubbery. Straight ahead, very close, is a building. It opens onto a great hall and, to the left, a stairwell. At a slight left, we find an entry where clothing is on display, together with other objects that cannot yet be identified. From the dishes that are carried and from the drinks that are served, which differ according to the time of day, one can see that the great hall is a café and a restaurant. But it's not merely a café, not merely a restaurant: in the middle stands a big fountain, from which no water springs but where rings of glass are enclosed in one another; they are fixed but look as if they were in motion. Further away there is a bar, framed from behind but with an overview by a wall with works on paper that, seen together, resemble a landscape. We look up and find porcelain branches falling from the ceiling, like stalactites.

We would take a turn and discover the clothing: fabrics adorning mannequins, suspended on hangers and racks, but also, further away, handbags, brooches, makeup, all kinds of objects. Certain objects are marked with letters that seem related to the place. We note brand names, but we see them in a big whole, coordinated with drawings in the background, with murals, with a large chandelier that hangs like a piece of vegetation. In the middle, people, visitors, and others are ready to present the objects, to describe them as if they were tourist guides, and to sell them.

A stairwell leads to the first floor; at the mezzanine, a little gallery, which on this day displays an installation; going further up, we bump into a bookstore: books of literature, art, photography, style, design, and then pens, pencils, and notebooks: the world of writing. Continuing along, we come to a larger gallery where photographs are on display. Through the windows we see the terrace replete with vegetation. We then decipher an inscription down below: 10 Corso Como.

I

Absolute Commerce

It's not merely commerce—and for banal reasons to begin with. The space, which has taken its address as its name, brings together different realities: a gallery, a bookstore, a store, a restaurant—and the list goes on. These spaces aren't simply juxtaposed, one beside the other, as they could be along one of these endless streets in any number of Italian or European centers. They aren't even disparate portions of a huge area, as they would be in a mall or in the commercial centers that have imitated and reproduced the urban landscapes of Italy. At 10 Corso Como each of these parts is a function and expression of something larger—something more homogeneous and more coherent than what we see in each one of them. The scene is not one of an experience that multiplies and diversifies, or one where the setting induces in the act of purchase a sense of contemplation, relaxation, or restauration. What we behold is a space of a limitless experience that no longer tolerates distinction. Paradoxical as it may seem, here is where *commerce is transformed into a space of total life*. That's exactly why the multiplication of spaces in no way follows the pattern of the city. On the contrary, it attempts to construct the exception, an island in which people and things can exist differently. It's a place where things can be encountered, notably objects from faraway places otherwise unavailable to the city's inhabitants; a place where the things that make our existence possible and livable can be encountered differently.

It's not merely commerce. In this space it is the very idea of commerce that has to transform itself, to put on a front unlike the one that has marked it over the centuries. We usually think of commerce as a necessary evil that makes exchange possible, a minimal form that space must take for the reason that objects can be sold and bought. Commerce is a limbo unworthy of memory, a center of temporary permanence in which commodities are stationed after being produced, where they remain before being conserved, a state of urgency from which objects must be liberated. Deprived of life and reality, commodities can only appear on the floor, display themselves in a shopwindow, be reduced to their own image only. But 10 Corso Como transforms the relation between space and object. It breaks the window asunder, opens it, turns it into the very body of commerce. Bodies, then, are like people: we meet them—we don't observe them. We spend time next to them and with them; they aren't simple objects within arm's reach. 10 Corso Como has dedicated to the encounter with things all the time and all the space it needs. We never enter a store only to buy things and carry them away; we enter in order to see them, touch them, smell them, spend time with them; we enter in order to meet them. At 10 Corso Como we literally live among things. We sleep there. The commercial establishment is no longer the uncertain border that isolates the exchange and makes it possible; nor is it the museum that isolates things outside exchange. Commerce is the forum of things, the space where we go to spend time with the objects that make our everyday lives possible.

It's not merely commerce. It's a city within the city or, better, it's a core born of a new urban model. No other commerce has sought to respond to the revolution that objects have wrought in the urban world. For more than a century, the aspect of the modern city has radically changed. All of a sudden telephones, cars, refrigerators, washing machines, television sets—but also new clothing, books, papers, tables, chairs, lamps, together with meats, vegetables, jewels, wrist watches—in sum, an infinite and for the most part unprecedented cohort of everyday objects has invaded the city, occupied domestic spaces, imposed itself as a privileged object of desire and attraction. It is not only new and unusual objects or objects generally rare to find within homes (washing machines, dishwashers, television sets, and now laptop computers) that irrupt into our households. It is above all the most usual, ordinary, banal objects, which multiply at an exponential rate—things like shoes, spaghetti, seats: everything today exists in tens of varieties, in hundreds of possible forms, in thousands of meticulously distinct modes of being. No single thing can be confused with another specimen with which it shares the same function and form. It is no longer a sweater, a

4

refrigerator, a table—but a Benetton or a Missoni sweater, a Frau armchair or a Kartell seat. Every single thing has acquired a name of its own that belongs to it alone, a blazon that testifies to its prestige in society. Every single thing is narcissistically absorbed in its own appearance and preoccupied to make visible its own value and its own longevity.

The invasion of things "thingifies" both the urban landscape and the political landscape. Today, in the city, the number and quality of things present exceeds those of men and women. The city and political space become a place where things are collected rather than one where people assemble. Commerce is, then, the true paradigm of political space. No longer is it the home or an aggregate of homes: political is, first and foremost, the space that allows people and things to meet one another, the space where each of the things produced, desired, sold, and acquired in the city becomes available to the totality of its inhabitants. On the other hand, political will be any space that makes *consumption* possible—the free, individual, and contingent relation people hold with things—and not the one that allows people to live side by side, in accordance with relations of kinship or unknown proximities. To choose the objects we wish to wear in public, to construct and establish a space in which they are accessible to all, to define the form of their public existence—all this means drawing a line between the borders and the face of the city, its habits and customs. 10 Corso Como has created a space where the most important and beautiful objects that humanity has produced—the first seeds of all things, the extreme perfection of human industry—are gathered, brought to life, and opened onto the world. It's where premises of all things are displayed. It has endowed the city with new inhabitants, has extended its borders and has changed the idea of a city center once and for all.

It's not merely commerce. It makes things exist in different ways, it allows commodities to be something other than the simple components of a commercial transaction. Things are the inhabitants and the structures of a space where one stops, where one eats, where one sleeps: distribution is not the missing or ungraspable link between production and consumption. It is the pivot of all this heterogeneous and contradictory sum of practices, ideas, objects, and portions of the world that we call economy. 10 Corso Como transforms the very idea of economy.

It's not merely commerce. It's the transfiguration of everything we've imagined that commerce could be. If we want to tell its story, we have to begin from afar. In this very place Carla Sozzani managed to bring together and express different histories, very far from one another, and at the same time to transform them profoundly. 10 Corso Como is also—and above all—the ultimate stage of a slow evolution that commerce witnessed in the West from the 1960s on. It is the most complete result of the revolution that she contributed to bringing to the fashion magazine, the most mature expression of all transformations that marketing and publicity have inspired in the idea of commodity. Recounting how and why 10 Como Corso came to be is to give a historical account of European culture and economy over the last decades. This is not a minor or local account of a small commercial province. It is the history of our global world and of the choices one could make of the things it imagines, produces, and consumes—its most beautiful and most precious part.

In 1990 Carla Sozzani founded 10 Corso

Como. The inauguration of this site devoted to creation occurred at a historic tipping point—local, national, and international—in the field of creative economy. It is from here that we must begin if we are to understand the scale of a project born of a transition. We can then take note of the successive stakes it entailed. For the founding was situated between two epochs, in a moment that was not yet the 1990s but had already passed the 1980s; and this straddling allowed it to operate a synthesis of the two, and hence to place itself beyond the limitations that come with too strong anchoring.

First of all, the name calls to mind a place. The name "10 Corso Como" coincides with that of an address—the name of a street, a destination, a voyage. Involved here is not an ordinary trajectory but a brief and intense pilgrimage. In full view at 10 Corso Como is not just a unique or special space, or Carla Sozzani's very personal and elegant universe, her obsessions, her taste, her intuitions. We go to 10 Corso Como for more ambitious ends: we go there to see—literally—what the ancients used to call the *world*.

The place is a presence. Real places, as real persons—persons who are alert, and therefore really human—surpass the status of a composite being, made up of fragments that can be counted, analyzed, and itemized, to become a kind of syncretic totality that can be called "a presence." A presence is the mark of life that gets affixed to an existing substance.

Plutarch tells us that, at the moment of the foundation of Rome, Romulus, following an ancient Etruscan ritual, threw the first seeds of all things into a hole that he then proceeded to fill. The hole, Plutarch says, had the same name as the universe: *mundus*.[1] At 10 Corso Como emphasis is placed on all the first seeds of the world—everything of the most beautiful and of the most unbelievable sort that has come to life, has appeared, and has been produced in the world. 10 Corso Como's name coincides with this space, a space that concentrates for us all the beauty that exists on the planet, a space that makes beauty exist in things, that wondrously transforms our earth into cosmos.

Carla Sozzani, in her previous life as an editor, has imposed an image of the woman, an image of fashion, even an image of the image. Over the years, every articulation of her vision has been strengthened; in the end, what she has established is an architecture of existence. This powerful woman, who published images of women by turns sensuous, strong, and timeless, is the person whose salient traits she herself—or at any rate an extension of herself—saw making their mark.

The name of 10 Corso Como is that of our *mundus*: it is present both among us and in the world, not as a simple conscience or a person. This presence is not only a gaze, a taste, an infinite knowledge cast upon things and their novelty. It is the force that makes beauty exist in things here and now.

This image and this fashion belong in a moment and push away its limits in order to enter a space of timelessness—being thus entirely of an era and entirely outside that era. They maintain the tension without making it the source of a negation: on the contrary, both emerge stronger. The moment obtains a duration it never had, and as a result its timelesness is grounded in its own reality. Carla Sozzani's proximity to Azzedine Alaïa, to Rei Kawakubo, to Ettore Sottsass, to Marc Newson, to Helmut Newton, to Sarah Moon, to Paolo Roversi, to Bruce Weber, and to so many others is a sign of a passion to live the present—

and life—all the more intensely as it carries in itself the roots of the past and the foundations of the future. All these designers and photographers have embedded within their work traces, references, and methods from the past, while pushing it to the most unexpected of places.

A shrewd detective, Carla Sozzani can find signs of vision everywhere, both in the moment and outside time; and she recognizes them in art, in photography, in fashion, in design, in literature. There is no field in which her particular criterion, so difficult to apply, both contemporary and timeless, does not manifest itself. The criterion itself defines expertise: she can play with everything, not only because she is an expert in these areas but especially because she masters the arcana of a vision that is not subjective but rather objective.

This capacity to bring together the most diverse and unexpected manifestations of beauty and make them live in the same place is the very faculty that allows her to build creative friendships with great visionaries of our time.

Subjectivity is often expressed in what is passing: at some point in our lives, we love something that we know will pass. As the saying goes, "it's just a fling." We know well that it can't last, that, as Proust's Swann would say, "it's not his type"—yet out of laziness, out of carelessness, we let ourselves go. That's the domain of the subjective. The new is subjective. It's limited.

On the other hand, the domain of objectivity is determined by a passion, an admiration, an act of giving oneself to an ideal, which lies outside ourselves: the objective puts itself before our eyes; it must be universal, as we see it, and we restrict ourselves to serving this ideal. Carla Sozzani says it often: speaking of her love of beauty, she says that she is there only to serve creators in all domains. By defining her role in this way, she relegates to silence the essential contribution she brings to their creations. But above all she emphasizes the objectivity of her vocation: she serves an object, her ideal, a certain idea of beauty, harmony, transcendence.

10 Corso Como is one of Carla Sozzani's many names: one of the forms that her personality has invented in order to make *mundus* exist in our time. But there are thousands of others. The place is a *mundus*, a space in which the ideas of beauty that have visited and will visit humanity are contained as if in a jewelry case that can be gazed at each time anyone speaks with her.

At stake here is not beauty as much as the sublime. From pseudo-Longinus to Barnett Newman, the sublime is defined as "the echo of a great soul"[2] that, by virtue of its greatness, makes us perceive in art its transcending nature; "in the fine arts man's nature desire [*sic*] is to express his relation with the absolute."[3] Carla Sozzani ceaselessly aspires to humanize the sublime: the sublime must not be an experience of disconnection, hierarchical, socially conditioned by the space of a museum. Today we need the sublime to continue to illuminate our lives as if it were a light shining from within. A response to this crisis bears the name 10 Corso Como. Carla Sozzani underlines it in her own words: "I wanted to make an art gallery where the works could be touched." Her remark is anything but indifferent, indeed it is reminiscent of Brâncuși's dream when he wanted his viewers to caress the surface of his works, and when he went as far as to conceive a series of *Sculptures for the Blind* in 1916.[4]

Throughout the 1980s, she played a considerable part in the change of the nature of fashion magazines. From being a simple seismograph— faithful but blind—obstinately limited to recording, season after season, variations in taste and in social appearances, much like a faintly colored atlas of a world destined to disappear before the first printing. Under her editorship, the special issues of *Vogue* and the Italian edition of *Elle* have become veritable organs of vision— more precisely, instruments of a unique utopia: namely, in a limited space of a few pages, she gathers together the most wondrous images and the most wondrous words about the most wondrous things, both present and future.

Her idea is that we must break away from the limitation of forms, which makes it right to qualify a given form of creation as sublime, but not another. This means creating a space stronger and greater even than a museum, in order to open the experience of the sublime to all forms of human creativity: a space that is what a museum ought to be, an atmosphere in which things will be accorded the force of art and thus will be able to stir, in each one, an experience of the order of those that lead one beyond oneself.

Corso Como has been the name of the quest for all forms of *mundus* that have yet to exist, of future worlds that she has explored. Exactly like the hero of Plato's myth of the cave, we are first to exit into the light and to discover that images correspond to things, even the images discovered and created for the place itself.

The experience of a visit to 10 Corso Como will persists in every memory; if a buyer purchases an object, no matter how insignificant it may be, he or she takes part in an experience of going beyond. In the face of consumerism, 10 Corso Como imposes upon clients the antidote of a vision from which they emerge inoculated, mithridatized, strengthened by the power of a vision.

Plutarch tells us that every city has to be able to found itself upon this little world. 10 Corso Como is not merely a concept store. *Vogue* and *Elle* were not merely monthlies. They are the *mundus* of our world, the world upon which she has founded a parallel city on the inner folds of Milan's urban fabric.

In the 1980s Milan witnessed an economic success until then unknown. It was the period of *Milano da bere* ["Milan to drink"], which invigorated everything Italian and is found in cinema, in literature, in journalism. The city turned itself into a center of fashion, of creation, of art, and of money. Rome, on the other hand, which had seen a tremendous surge of energy in the post-war years until the 1960s and even in the 1970s, progressively began to fall asleep. Likewise Turin, where artists had congregated through the 1960s and 1970s, had now been turned into a backwater.

Through her editorial duties, through the relations that she held with photographers, creators, and designers both Italian and international, Carla Sozzani was a central figure of this moment in which Milan was in the process of becoming a center of the world of creation. Throughout Italy she helped build the careers of artists with whom she was still working three decades later. She sided with the artists and allowed them to enter the world. She was the guardian at the portal of a universe access to which had become desirable to everyone.

A new generation of fashion magazines and tendencies emerged in the 1970s. Even traditional magazines such as *Vogue* changed their editorial policies radically: from simple gazettes of international clothing style that cared for the feminine image, they turned into organs of periodic visual inquiry into the ambient material culture. Every issue stops being a collection of possible modes of dress and purchase advices and makes itself into a printed museum of objects and images originating from the world of fashion, of design, of gastronomic research, of cinema, of books. The magazine becomes a space for the collection and study of style, conceived of as a family resemblance that permeates all things: not only objects recognized as art on formal and academic grounds, but all the objects that populate public and private space. In turn, the very idea of material culture, as the store had forged it and academic anthropology was trying to define it, underwent a further transformation: at stake was no longer a culture assimilated or acquired, but one imagined and imaginary. From a certain standpoint the magazine represents the phase of ultimate achievement, in the twentieth century, of culture as material culture, a state in which culture recovered its status of shared imagination. On the other hand, from the 1980s on, the magazines are, even more than the stores, the true driving force of global material culture.

Carla Sozzani has been one of the great protagonists in this story. Having begun by working for *Vogue Italia* in the mid-1970s, she graduated in modern languages from Bocconi University and immediately afterwards embarked on a collaboration with those who were to become the greatest fashion photographers at the end of the twentieth century: Robert Mapplethorpe, Sarah Moon, Herb Ritts, Paolo Roversi, Deborah Turbeville, Wegman and Bruce Weber. To borrow the title of a famous New York exhibition related to the 1990s, this season can be summed up as the attempt to turn photographic fiction into the very medium of fashion making. Fashion photography stops portraying the model as a piece of abstract, surrealist still life that highlights the product—clothing, accessories—to become the narrative of a mysterious and not always comprehensible story, whose object is a form of life, a style, a mode of being—and the object of that is only a vehicle and incarnation. The series of photographic expositions assembled over the years at 10 Corso Como was to be, at once, the expression and the cause of this deep investigation, narrative and existential, of contemporary photography. The role of this concept store in the diffusion and disclosure of the photographic art in Italy is enormous.

Carla Sozzani took leave of *Vogue Italia*'s special issues to become the editor-in-chief of Italian *Elle* in 1987. She would have time to publish only three issues—now legendary—which have played a most important role in international fashion publishing. She collaborated with the greatest photographers of the era, from formal figures such as Sarah Moon, Peter Lindbergh, Bruce Weber, Paolo Roversi, and Steven Meisel to the new ones that define the 1990s—including Nick Night and Jürgen Teller. She decided to be rid entirely of the commercial side of things in order to create spaces of visual inspiration: she associated with Robin Derrick, who had worked for *I-D* and *The Face*; and she opened the magazine to fashion and to international design, at a time when the label "Made in Italy" was turning from myth into a marketing strategy designed to conserve a drained patrimony. At stake, as Cathy Horyn had written, was "an aesthetic interruption in the direction of a magazine, something rare in its beauty and its influence." The birth of 10 Corso Como— an umpteenth instance of the heterogenesis of aims—is due to her abrupt and inexplicable dismissal from the editorship of Italian *Elle*. In Carla Sozzani's words, the goal was, with her new venture, to "create a magazine in a different way, to express the same thing I had been doing with the magazines, but from life itself."[5] 10 Corso Como was the project of a tridimensional magazine, a sort of collage and installation *in vivo* of entities simultaneously commercial, cultural, and visual. "Its pages were becoming walls, shelves, and tables; its readers were becoming clients." Also at stake, in this instance, was a movement of radicalization. Material culture, which had conquered once more a space of purely visual imagination through the magazine, was coming back to make itself into a world, a living space, a place of life, material time.

1990 was different from the 1980s: preparations were made to enter into a new decade. The luxury, the sumptuousness of life that prevailed in the 1980s were already beginning to fade; in the 1990s, they declined. Milan was no exception: the more this city had grown in the preceding decade, the more it repositioned itself in the 1990s: money, flowing to a point that had gone beyond measure in the 1980s, became scarce. Its use had to find legitimacy. Hereafter the gratuity of spending was no longer a worthy alibi.

The 1990s were the years in which Europe's economic lethargy deepened. The luxury industry, of which 10 Corso Como was part, needed to find a new place in society. Extravagance was no longer a value in itself. Art could no longer be sold at astronomical prices, as happened in the 1980s when the fame of artists such as Jean-Michel Basquiat, Francesco Clemente, Eric Fishl, David Salle, Julian Schnabel had created a speculative bubble. From that point on art, the art of life, hieratic creation, all had to defend their place in the market and in the city.

During the 1980s Milan had become more than ever an international city linked to Paris, New York, London, and Tokyo. A cosmopolis was sprawling across countries and constituted its own horizon for creation. Carla Sozzani had spent a good deal of time in New York in the 1980s and had learned its lessons. New York was a city whose margins had become brutally central. Greenwich Village, SoHo, Tribeca, later on Chelsea, and finally Brooklyn, which in the 1980s were shady places populated with garages, nightclubs, and sex stores, had been absorbed by the world of art and creation, which made them into its theater before entering directly into speculation. In such places—uncared for, often dilapidated, made of concrete, with exposed stone, with rickety stairwells, with cracked sidewalks—people felt astonishingly at ease with life; perhaps it was becoming more responsive to them.

The urban horizon changed: this New York feeling that what was beautiful didn't have to be perfect, that what was ultra-chic did not have to be order and tradition—that was alien to Europe. In Milan everyone spoke only of the golden quadrilateral. In Paris, the Marais neighborhood emerged thanks to the presence of the Centre Pompidou. In London it was only toward the end of the 1990s that the urban structure changed, through integration with the financial market of East London.

Carla Sozzani has drawn all the consequences from this situation and from the opportunities it offered. She has extracted the substance from the sites of creation and life in New York and has transformed them into a place dedicated to the presentation and diffusion of the same creation— a place of commerce. This was 10 Corso Como. As she puts it herself, "the neighborhood was lost: amid fruit sellers and hardware stores." That she chose such an area attests to an awareness that the urban equilibrium, in Milan as in other locales of this western cosmopolis, was about to change.

The impact of money and societal transformation were to lead to a larger inclusion of neighborhoods than ever before; the absorption that had taken place in New York was inevitable and, just as in the United States, it was up to the field of creation to get it going. The new space filled this role. The very fact that the place had taken its address to be its name signaled that 10 Corso Como was a manifesto: it was possible to open a place of creation in that very spot in the city. And the sole fact that it had existed proved that times were changing and that a new era had begun.

When 10 Corso Como was conceived, it opened first of all as a photography gallery, then a windowless store with a cement floor, at a time when every store in Milan had windows and a marble floor. In contrast to what was done then for the sake of selling the goods—and those were the days when the buyer had to be satisfied in every way, so as to feel at ease and be able to acquire the object with an impression of gregarious luxury—Carla Sozzani tilted the new setting in the direction of creation—no shopwindows, a cement floor: the store could be an artist's studio.

The fact that the place had originally been dedicated to photography and clothing can also be interpreted as a sign of awareness of the challenges of the time: in the 1980s, as Dave Hickey stressed, photography had been rising as a medium.[6] In moving from fashion photography to what was called "art" photography, the field of photography had marked its own identity with specific traits: the treatment of light, the place left for the human face, the use of modern techniques or, on the contrary, the intention to remain within the historical modalities of form. Carla Sozzani, who had worked with many photographers and taken part in the birth of the careers of Steven Meisel, David LaChapelle, Patrick Demarchelier, Peter Lindbergh, Paolo Roversi, and Bruce Weber, who had been very close to Helmut Newton, had a new approach to photography: she conceived of a photography that exists in itself, as art, and no longer suffers from some crisis of legitimacy. The kind of photography that interests her just is and never calls itself in question; a formed language, it perfects itself and moves forward.

In the same fashion, in the 1980s clothing had entered into a new era: the inaugural rupture between haute couture and prêt-à-porter was mended. Until then the common idea related to the fact that, since the 1950s and more so with Pierre Cardin and Yves Saint-Laurent Rive Gauche, the prêt-à-porter had opened a breach. It popularized a universe of style that had previously belonged only to the cream of the elite. Hence there was a basic suspicion that the prêt-à-porter was a mere surrogate of couture, a vulgarization and, as Benjamin's theory of art would have it, a loss of aura.

The 1980s swept this suspicion aside. Even before the beginnings of 10 Corso Como, great voices of the decade, from Azzedine Alaïa to Rei Kawakubo, who were both very close to Carla Sozzani, made it clear that the gap no longer existed; that it was possible (and more important even) to make clothing into a unique horizon, without any hierarchy or separation between couture and prêt-à-porter, and to develop the potential of clothing in such a way that it enters the stores and does not remain the exclusive reality of a privileged few, as a result of structural factors. Azzedine Alaïa, whose work was accompanied by photography all the way from Bill Cunningham to Paolo Roversi, conceived of clothing beyond the divide between couture and prêt-à-porter. In a word, Carla Sozzani made couture an element of everyday life.

Thus this sense of community between couture and photography, both of them pillars of Carla

Sozzani's creative work, reveals an assumption of her project: creating the place most suitable for two media that had undergone the test of popularization without getting lost but had emerged from it even stronger, more sharply defined, and more dominant than they had been before.

On the one hand, this elaboration was, then, the result of a democratization: painting was not initially on display at 10 Corso Como and was only rarely later on, and sculpture remained a marginal element in programming. Sculpture and painting, hierarchical modes of art, were for the most part excluded from the program. At the same time, what had been democratized was—through its own quality and ambition— caught in a perspective of innovation. This was not photography made by just anybody: it was Man Ray, Elgort, La Chapelle, Meisel, Leibovitz, Rober Ballen, Lindbergh, Guy Bourdin, Newton, Rodchenko, and many more. Nor was it common couture: it was Alaïa and Comme des Garçons, Martin Margiela's first collection.

The point was to get to the heart of the matter—namely the problem of hierarchies— and to act on the oscillations that had come into daylight in order to mark the entry into a new era of resolution. That was a site where poetic, creative activity was taking place; one had to stitch up the conflicts of domination between this form and that, between this horizon and that. It was a working-class neighborhood, far away from everything. It was also a metaphor for the terrain that Carla Sozzani was opening for herself—a metaphor for her seeking a renewal of creative work in that opening, for her stepping out of the isolation that threatened the fertility of a period of intense life.

In 1991, right at the beginning of the decade, Galleria Carla Sozzani—the exhibition section of 10 Corso Como—had organized an exhibition entitled "Espressioni dell'arte degli anni '90" ["Expressions of the Art of the 1990s"]. This exhibition, which took an active interest in very original creators—among them, already, Kris Ruhs—was a manifesto: one had to show that the space in the process of developing had a good hold on the decade that had hardly begun. As of 1991, the Galleria indicated that it was interested in irreducible singularities and attempted, with the help of these singularities, to seize a moment that was nevertheless still in the future for the most part.

The entire spirit of the project was revealed in that exhibition: the Galleria, just like 10 Corso Como, of which it was part, inherited from the 1980s a taste for individuality, whereas the 1990s, especially in art, built more around collaboration, around the idea of the group—this diffuse "avant-garde that was not an avant-garde," which Olivier Zahm mentions with reference to the artists of the "decade,"[7] namely that of Martin Margiela, Dominique Gonzalez-Foerster, Philippe Parreno, and Pierre Huyghe. At the same time the Galleria asserted that these figures were making it possible to understand the art of a period—the genitive in *l'arte degli anni '90* [the art of the 1990s] rather than the locative in *l'arte negli anni '90* [the art in the 1990s]—and thus to enter in this decade one way or another. At stake here was not art, not fashion, not design, not photography; it was the moment itself and how it could be grasped, on the one hand by those who had designed the site and its programming, on the other, remotely, by those who visited it.

In consequence, many components that seemed scattered or disjointed at a first glance became crystallized in this project. In the mix were the political and economic future of Italy and Milan's urban scene; creative cosmopolitism and a keen sense of place; an unshakeable faith in the work of art and cessation of the supremacy of the traditional media of painting and sculpture; the legacy of the 1980s and a direct orientation toward the decade to come.

This crystallization was already turning 10 Corso Como—as well as its founder—into a center of thinking with many points of entry and with far higher stakes than the exclusive packaging of a store: it was a problem area, a site where questions were raised, doubling the reality of the sale of objects.

The last great revolution that 10 Corso Como imposes upon our experience of things relates to the nature of the brand. From a strictly material point of view, the origins of branding coincide with those of human culture: the use of signs, of strokes, of marks made to define the symbolic separation of property and the ranking of personal objects is an archaic practice, for it is the specific form of that sociability to which human beings attribute their origin. Thus the relation of reciprocal implication between the brand and commerce is not an exclusive attribute of capitalist economy: on the contrary, it is a much older phenomenon than we might be led to believe.

In criticizing the traditional position of economic history, according to which primitive commodities are represented by natural, unworked products such as wheat, cotton, and potatoes, which can be replaced by an equivalent of any kind, anthropologists have demonstrated that the introduction of marks is the first condition for the structuring of a complex market, different from the primitive model of the bazaar.[8] In an unstructured market (the bazaar), everything is uncertain: the true nature of the object put up for sale and its "biography" (provenance, history, mode of production, quality) are neither evident nor legible on the skin and surface of the commodity; hence the relation with the object and all the information pertaining to it must be mediated by the seller. The introduction of brand names and of trademarks permits in the first place to correct and balance "the asymmetry of information between buyer and the seller" and to build a sort of shared cognitive map with the help of which the origin of the commodity can be traced and its quality foreseen. In this way it is not only that "efficient channels of communication between producers and consumers" are produced "which are independent of the chain of intermediary traders and middlemen,"[9] but also that the nature of market competition changes, evolving "from the relationship between buyer and seller to the relationship between sellers."[10] It is still the symbolic marking or branding of commodities that transforms the market into a "public" space where the secret becomes impossible, in opposition

> to the excessive secretiveness of the bazar which both grows out of and is seeded with suspicion. Where the bazar trader is obsessed with secrecy and with protecting business information on his sources of supply the size of his inventory and of his clientele, the standardized commodity trader advertises his comprehensive range of stock, the producers from whom he purchases, and the size of his clientele.[11]

Confirming and radicalizing Faselow's intuitions, David Wengrow has shown not only that the use of branding existed in Mesopotamian civilization, but that the use of standardized sealed packaging gave rise to an economy in which commodity and labor could easily replace each other.[12] The brand is what allows an object to be turned into a commodity; in this sense, it hosts the attempt to resolve "a paradox common to ancient and modern economies of scale: the reincorporation of homogenous goods into a world of complex personal relationships"[13] or, better, "the realities of living in a community of individual actors formed and sustained through the circulation of impersonal objects."[14]

The origin of brands, as we know them today, is to be found at the end of the nineteenth century, but it was especially from the 1950s on that they acquired the importance we are in the habit of giving them today.[15] In contrast to common belief, a brand will completely restructure its own market when consumption stops being exclusively defined by the desire to display or confirm one's social superiority or status (according the logic of Veblen's conspicuous consumption), or on the other hand by the will to mimic that of the upper classes, in bovarist manner (this would be Gabriel Tarde's social mimetism). It is only when consumption ceases to be defined by socially determined variants that it becomes necessary to associate a product with an array of extremely complex meanings, values, and emotions, of which the brand is at once the seal and the ultimate signifier.[16] Precisely because the relation that prompts individuals to produce, to acquire, and to use objects, especially certain objects and not others, is much more complex and profound,[17] the symbolic mark through which the object is given to be known and recognized not only acquires more importance, but must carry much more information than it had before. For this very reason, from this moment on, the brand will not limit itself to structuring the market and making possible a more balanced flow of information between buyer and seller. Above all, it will have to carry the object and to incorporate in it a much greater amount of significance and meaning than it had in the past. The brand is no longer "the label employed to differentiate the various manufacturers of a product," but becomes "a complex symbol that represents a variety of ideas and attributes."[18] It is through this sensitive symbol that things speak. It is through this self-image that every piece of merchandise coincides with a "public image."[19]

Observed on a global scale (and not on a single product), branding is a classification of the objects of this world, or of groups of objects, which operates not through purely logical or social categories but through sensible, nonmimetic, and not purely linguistic signs. Once these have been affixed to the things they signify, they allow each thing not only to distinguish itself from the rest of the objects produced and exchanged but also to convey a potentially infinite and extremely complex series of socially shared meanings. It is not enough to produce, distribute, buy, or sell things; it is necessary to support the commodities with symbols, to organize them, to parcel up the reality of objects and producers with the help of these symbols, to set up the sensible appearance of the world by means of these visible signs. If this series of symbols allows us to arrange the objects and, derivatively on them, also the persons who produce and those who acquire them, this order has nothing divine and nothing natural either: it is contingent and mobile and must favor the mobility and contingency of things, their circulation—in other words the sum of those effects that we label "commercial." By presupposing an activity of *branding*, then, the market reveals itself to be a form of primitive aesthetic arrangement, a kind of first cosmic categorization that permits on the one hand the *socialization* of the world of things (these can pass from hand to hand and are not tied to a single subject) and, on the other, the liberation of things, which are then capable of circulating without having to be mediated by a subject-person in order to establish themselves qua recognizable, appropriable, and usable. The brand is what allows things to be known through themselves.

Branding tells us that every market is a cosmological fact even before being a social fact. On the one hand, the market is not a reality that follows the composition of the world and of society: rather it enables a society to construct a world qua moving reality, produced, and not just given to us in order that we contemplate and know it (the market, too, is in some way presupposed, so that things may be produced and desired). The array of categories that accompany the structuring of the social body is of an aesthetic rather than a logical nature. It is not only a name but also a logo, a perceptible reality; it is not a pure logical or semiotic reality, but a nonanalogous image added to the thing. Through branding, then, every society redoubles the world *aesthetically*—but not *logically* or linguistically—

in order to transform it into a set of things that can be passed from hand to hand; it is no longer a pure object of contemplation. If *socialization* foresees and implies a logical arrangement of the real, *commercial release* anticipates and involves an aesthetic display, an aesthetic construction of the world and its objects, their duplication and perceptible distribution.

The coincidence between art and the marketplace that seals the brand is important for at least two other reasons. First, it allows us to extend the very idea of an aesthetic dimension of things; and what represents it is no longer the sphere in which they are objects of contemplation, but the condition of possibility of their circulation. Second, here the symbol displays a different status from the one we usually confer upon it. A brand is an incomplete symbol because it cannot signify on its own; in every instance it has to be affixed to the thing itself in order to signify something and hence be able to complete its own meaning. On the other hand, it represents a new relation between thing and object: insofar as it is inseparable from its brand, a piece of merchandise is an object that defines itself through its own symbol, which is stamped upon it. By virtue of branding, things are defined on the basis of their own aesthetic symbol.

10 Corso Como seems to bring two paradigms together: it applies the model of the *bazaar* to the world of brands. From a certain standpoint, this is a reaction to the recent development of the market: the multiplication of brands, the explosion in the production of luxury, the extreme diversification of patterns of consumption, the desire to look for local products of quality have all led us back to a primitive situation where consumers face a mass of commodities whose nature and quality they cannot understand. The concept of store makes brand and commerce coincide, transforming the act of buying into a total aesthetic experience. This is the same development we witnessed in the art world with Documenta 5, when Harald Szeemann organized the first exposition, titled *conceptual, in*, in which the secondary auctoriality* of the *curator* replaced that of the artist.

* Fr. *auctorialité*, a coinage that inserts the idea of authority into the term "author" by alluding to the latter's Latin ancestor, *auctor*.

2

The Eternal and the Ephemeral

Collection is the act farthest from creation. First of all, from a chronological point of view: it takes place when everything that could be created has already been developed. It arises when the last spark of creation is extinguished. It takes place after the exhaustion of all available energies. It marks the end of all things and all actions, even of silence and of emptiness.

It is the act farthest from creation. And it is so from a historical point of view as well: it is a tendency opposed to any development, a gesture that shuts history once and for all. It is the movement that puts an end to the cycles of birth and death, the idea that brakes the wheels of loss and return.

It is the act farthest from creation. And it is so especially from a metaphysical point of view: to choose, to select—that is a gesture diametrically opposed to the movement that allows a subject to produce or engender. Collection never lays hands on forms. It is not animated by concern for what might emerge, but rather by what *must* vanish or what *must* be eliminated. It produces waste, it aims at the oblivion of what exists.

It is the act farthest from creation. And yet it is only thanks to it that there can be art. For centuries we have celebrated creation as what is most sublime in the human being. And yet without the desire to collect—in other words, the desire to create a fundamental difference between castaways and survivors—all creation would be no more than the painfully automatic reproduction of what there is. Without a judgment that recognizes the work of art amid a series of objects, without the act that physically separates it from other spaces, from other objects, from other possible uses, everything would be condemned to collapse into its own function. This is not simply a sociological matter; the question is that creation is never sufficient for the production of art. Granted, there would be no art in our society if there were no artists; but it is only in our judgment that art exists qua art. Nor is it a matter of exhuming the romantic superiority of criticism over poetry. For it is only in the activity of collecting, and not in critical activity, that the judgment encounters and molds reality; it is only in a collection and through collecting that a thing becomes a work of art. It matters little whether we are dealing with a museum or with a private domestic treasure.

Carla Sozzani is not a simple collector. She has not limited herself to accumulating, over time, various objects that should testify to the nature of her taste, to her encounters, to her intellectual adventures. Nor has she become invested in the attempt to elevate the activity of collecting by tying it to other ends than itself (knowledge or dissemination, philanthropy, politics). In her hands, collecting has stopped being a marginal, elitist, and eccentric cultural practice to reveal a deeper nature, radical and primeval: that of a mechanism of individuation and generation, not only of art, but of any cultural object and fact. The collection is only the physiology, the breath of what German idealism had called the objective spirit. Besides, the word "collection" could make a perfect rendering of ancient Greek *logos*—a word that conveys the idea of reason, spirit, and intelligence.

Collecting is the life of the soul. To know is always an act of collecting: to relate to the world always means grasping images, and every image is but a collection of the real—in the double meaning of something that we have chosen, detached, and separated from the continuum of colors and forms on display before our eyes, but also of something we would wish to carry with us. Conversely, every collection of images is a spiritual and eminently cultural form: to gather and display images on the same surface is not to produce an inert album but means ipso facto imposing upon the collective mind a movement or a change. To collect images *periodically* signifies imprinting on mind and thought a completely unprecedented rhythm of change and development.

It was in this frame of mind that Carla Sozzani contributed to revolutionizing the fashion press. It is thanks to her and her peers that, from the 1980s on, fashion magazines stopped being gazettes exclusively dedicated to feminine clothing and its forms in order to open to the totality of human artifacts. The magazine became

the official space of visual communication: tex-
tual matter was reduced, images were the ones
designed to communicate. But the collection of
images did not respond to the rhapsodic logic
of a kind of iconic *Wunderkammer* [cabinet of
curiosities]. Every issue became an instrument for
harvesting style and for doing research on it—on
style, conceived of as a family resemblance that
envelops all things, not only the objects officially
recognized as art, but all objects that populate
private and public space. Thus it was the very idea
of art that found itself transformed: an object's
capacity to make beauty exist was no longer tied
either to a medium or to some specialized technical discipline (painting, cinema, sculpture).
Any substrate and any object could become an
object of art, in other words could get a place
in this collection of images on paper, which is
nothing but an avant-garde form of the museum.
On the other hand, by renewing the tradition
of Diane Vreeland and Alexey Brodovich at
Harper's Bazaar and of Alexander Liberman at
Vogue, Carla Sozzani surrounded herself with
the best photographers of the moment for the
sake of bringing a new language to the pages of
her magazines—a language liberated both from

strictly documentary obligations (because fashion photography had no obligation to submit to the obsession with evidence for "it was so and so") and from the metadiscursive or supremely critical pretensions of contemporary visual art. And this new photographic language, which would be that of our modernity, profoundly changed publicity and public communication. "Bound" to pay heed to clothing, accessories, and objects of everyday use, photography ceased staging an object as still life and turned instead into a true story told through images, a story in which clothes were the narrators rather than the protagonists. It was in the pages of Carla Sozzani's magazines that our world and our society learned how to make the photographic image not only a major art but also a privileged and paradigmatic form of self-consciousness. It was in these magazines that photography became not only an instrument of knowing or witnessing what is happening around us, but the main tool for constructing a world qua collection of everything that is worthy of our gaze and that, precisely for this reason, has a right to survive in collective memory. The collection is at once the invisible watermark and the secret scaffolding of this profound transformation that

Carla Sozzani has triggered through her editorial practice, which was part of a movement that changed for good the role of the photographic image in our lives.

When we reflect on 10 Corso Como, one of the most pressing questions that arise concerns its status. What is it? A store? A concept store—in line with the name that the sociologist Francesco Morace coined for it in 1991? Yes. "A magazine in the real world," as Carla Sozzani described it in her own words? Besides, who is Carla Sozzani? What is her function? Is she a businesswoman? An editor-in-chief at the head of a new genre of publication? A collector? The three answers can support one another but hardly allow us to grasp, even in a piecemeal way, the nature of her activity—and the nature of 10 Corso Como, which is so much an intrinsic part of it.

By liberating the store from its functionalist reduction to the *Existenzminimum* [minimum subsistence level] of exchange, 10 Corso Como transforms it into a privileged space through which style, human beings, and things no longer stand separate and in opposition to one another. Only in this prolonged and reiterated encounter do we succeed in recognizing a style and in developing a sense for it. Such is exactly the goal of the store: to display and make possible the existence of style, but also to make style accessible, a something that is unique not only to things (to the work of art), but to individuals as well. A store is in the first place the manifestation of style, of the power of things; only in the store can the power of things manifest itself.

Pop art had made commodities as such—their status, their aesthetics, their relation with works of art—its privileged target. *American Supermarket* had transformed and intensified this reflection on the store as store—the unique space in which the commodity exists qua commodity and neither as object of production (as it is in the factory) nor as object of consumption and use (as it becomes in people's homes, once its purchase has taken place). Being a market, the store seems, then, to exist within and beyond, before and after the simple fact of the economic transaction around a specific object.

This coincidence between the store and the gallery indicates to what point the store is the site of a pure and total display of things, a space in which things are revealed in their most perceptible nature. Rather the display of things loses its purely commercial finality: the shopwindow is an arrangement that invites contemplation but not seduction. We can no longer think of the display as something external to the commercial arrangement of things and posterior to it. The display becomes the deepest economic force, economy becomes synonymous with aesthetics, and the store seems to be the purest and most primitive encounter with things, within and beyond exchange.

That had already been the claim of the avant-garde at the beginning of the twentieth century: "the shopwindow is an important part of the general appearance of our cities. The storekeeper uses it as an artist and not as a mediator,"[1] wrote Friedrich Naumann. And in an overlooked book, published in 1939, Friedrick Kiesler (who had previously been part of the De Stijl movement) was thinking of the shopwindow as the summation of all the arts. It was Kiesler who first announced: "We will have no more walls."[2] The shopwindow is not simply the outer threshold of the store; rather it is the incarnation of its deeper essence. The store is the form of existence of culture in the new century, the one and only form that allows the arts to reach the public and the masses.

Since the 1960s the shopwindow has become, remarkably, a world of its own through the extraordinary inventiveness that Leila Menchari deployed for Hermès from 1978 to 2013,[3] but also with the help of the "windows" of great English and American department stores—Barneys in New York, Harvey Nichols and Harrods in London. Storefronts have become windows for creation and dream arrangements, in which objects available for sale are integrated into the present transformation of striking images. In the case of Hermès, these open-ended worlds in a closed container—the store window—have become a signature that is felt and recognized by generations of onlookers. As for 10 Corso Como, the windows there are on the inside.

And here resides the propensity of commodities to mutate—here, in this coincidence between the store and the gallery. Commodities have ceased to be the crystallization of labor; on the contrary, the gallery seems to be a crystallized form of the marketplace. This purification or "aesthetic reduction" is something in which time plays a fundamental role. In 1985 Andy Warhol stated: "Close a department store today, open it a hundred years later, and you'll have an art museum." As we know, twenty years later, this miracle already took place: organized at the Tinguely Museum in Basel, the exhibition titled "Das grosse Stilleben: Le petit Grand-Magasin" staged a department store in Mugron, in the south of France, that had remained intact for about thirty years after its closing.[4] It would seem that what makes a store entirely "commercial," what conceals its profoundly aesthetic nature, is its relation with the present. We could thus reverse Warhol's diagnostic by saying that the store is not a museum without a past, but a museum that prefers time to history.

Any store seems blend with the institution of the museum, but with several important differences: it conserves and at the same time transforms, just as the museum actualizes (in a process of overcoming itself).

In a museum, the principal function of displaying artifacts is to bring about and intensify a sensory, affective, and intellectual experience construed as a goal. The goal of the display is a sensory and mental actualization of the objects, which are, so to speak, summed up in and entirely absorbed by their pure appearance. No other use is possible, nor is any kind of interaction: the object cannot be integrated into the living world of any other subject and cannot build a personal biography. Once it is placed in a museum, an object is condemned to exist in a sort of acosmic interval in which, separated from its use and from its existence, it neither lives nor dies. It is as if the object were reified and materialized in the experience of display and contemplation. From this point of view the museum represents the most complete structure of abstraction. A store on the other hand is a mechanism intended to produce the opposite result: if the museum takes the object out of the world, the store is what opens the object onto *all possible worlds*. A store is not a catalogue of possible worlds, but an opening onto objects of *all* the possible worlds of those who could acquire them. For this reason the display in a commercial establishment does not have purely contemplative goals and the material reality of the object is not summed up in its appearance: its task is to suggest a sketch of the world that the acquisition of the object can liberate.

If the museum is a machine capable of producing a void in the ambient world, an acosmic interval in the worldly continuum of objects, actions, words, and events, the commercial establishment has to condense in the objects on display the possible transformations that the ambient world (and the worlds of the lives of the subjects who enter into contact with the object) will undergo. In a display it's not enough to set forward in a pure form every quality and every meaning embodied in the object itself: one must also make visible the forms in which this subject will itself structure the world and the sensory experience of the subject who will appropriate it. From this angle, a store is like a sum of indeterminate and nascent cosmogonies that will flourish only when the object will have left this floor. On the other hand, the store produces a strange cosmological inversion: a world is not what precedes the sum of the objects, but the twist that each object produces in a preexisting world as soon as it enters into contact with it.

A museum underscores and reinforces the autonomy of the object, in other words its separation from the rest of the objects and subjects that make up the cosmos. A store is a space in which the object can become the zenith of heteronomy: what the display must make visible is the capacity to enter into different worlds or, better, into *any possible world*, not only by adapting oneself to *each of them* but also by making each of them at once different and special. A store is not there to isolate the things of the world but to produce an intermediary world and to enable its insertion into any individual world.

If the museum is a cave that promises illumination, the store remains paradoxically faithful to the Platonic myth: it sets clients or buyers in a condition where they exit the cave knowing that the real world is the one that opens outside the store.

If the museum is essentially the incarnation of the universality of public space in opposition to what is private, the store seems to be an intermediary and indeed hybrid space that reconfigures the topology of cohabitation. It is not an *entirely* private space because any one can enter, and property is shown to be purely contingent and transitory. But neither is it not a public space either: one finds in it no pretense of universality, no wish to renounce individuality.

In order for new objects to be continually produced and for the things produced to be able to circulate, to be sufficiently desirable to pass from one hand to another, one must see the world as a property and emanation of the things themselves, from which something can be appropriated and is immediately communicable through their appearance. The store is the operator of this objectivation (in the sense of a reduction of the world to the echo of an object), of this multiplication and sensory composition of the cosmos. Through the store, the marketplace coincides with this same operation of reduction and sensory intensification of the world.

Many elements of the boutique can be found in 10 Corso Como. To be sure, the selection and formal layout may recall a magazine; but when you lay out objects on the page you don't work on paper, you work in space: you don't publish as much as you expose. And there are three kinds of place where you can do this: it can be a gallery—and there is after all the Galleria Carla Sozzani at 10 Corso Como, but that is only a part of the whole and not the whole itself—the same as Carla Sozzani Editore. It can also be an art center devoted to exhibitions of different natures. 10 Corso Como is surely a place where objects of different origins and realities are on display. However, the proliferation of these objects and their diversity make it difficult to put everything under the neat label "art center," all the more as the place obviously has a lot more than the resources of an art center in which works are presented and then withdrawn; there is of course a restaurant, a residential site, and a garden.

At this stage a conclusion would be possible: 10 Corso Como is neither a boutique, nor a gallery, nor an art center. It's a "concept store" whose model is by definition irreducible and, in the words of Franceso Morace, emanates only from itself. Corso Como is, to Corso Como, its own norm, its own "concept," which bears "a style of cultural selection, a philosophy of life and a unique vision of the world."[5] An approach of this sort has its own truth because, after all, it involves a person's vision, expressed in a specific place; certainly, then, this "unique" character has a role to play. Yet, as Carla Sozzani remarks herself, "unique" is the word that has become the least unique; and this unicity exists only insofar as it is a counterpoint to the institution that, in the western world, inclines most in the direction of the collective: the museum. It follows that the museum becomes—again, in the words of Francesco Morace—a "museum of beauty."

What is a museum? First of all, a museum is a place where things are presented: things presumed to be destined to last and be on call to nourish the public's mind. This is certainly the case with 10 Corso Como: here is the heart of the matter and the point that marks the break with the art center and the gallery, and clearly with the boutique. Most often—and especially when they deal with contemporary elements, as is the case here—these last three forms are dedicated to presenting the latest creations—in art, in style, in bookmanship, in all genres of production.

As soon as things are presented there, this carries an inherent assertion that they are destined to last: a book that is in the bookstore, a dish that is on the menu, a piece of clothing that makes its appearance, a set of photographs or design pieces that show up, all are in that place only because they are legitimized through their durability. This is often manifest in their aspect, which, albeit very audacious sometimes, does not belong to any period: whether it is a garment by Azedine Alaïa or by Comme des Garçons, a tomato pasta dish, a photographic album or a philosophy book, futurist works or an installation by Kris Ruhs, all these elements share a common point. At the moment when they are presented, they have already surpassed the age in which they exist, in order to attain a constructed timelessness—which is a kind of surpassing or *Aufhebung*.

In the same fashion, 10 Corso Como has created an aesthetics of black and white, which is evident in clothes of the 10 Corso Como brand—as the place manufactures its own creations—and in related accessories—pens, notebooks, handbags, and so on. Every one of these objects belongs to a simple aesthetics, which asserts itself without taking itself seriously. In the series of definitions of graphic design, it is situated in the 1980s and 1990s; at the same time, this efficacity refuses localization within a latest fashion.

This timelessness is also a form of universality, which is just as constructed and belongs just as much to a given moment: things are timeless in a precise moment and the museum, which gives its visitors a dizzying sense of time, does so in a totally different manner in 1800, in 1900, in 1930, in 2000, in 2020. Everything on display at 10 Corso Como is at once anchored with great precision in the heart of its moment—such and such a book, fresh from the press; one of Maurizio Cartelan's installations (look over there), a recent expression of his and Pierpaolo

Ferrari's vision—and exists in its own order. 10 Corso Como is extremely local—it is a quintessentially Milanese place—and yet all the places on the planet can be found inside; if we take a good look, the entire world is contained between the articles of clothing, the traces of foods, the program of exhibitions, and the books. This is notably the case with World Press Photo, the international photojournalism competition that the Galleria Carla Sozzani stages every year as an overture to what is happening everywhere, part of this universality she retranscribes.

If 10 Corso Como has a museal type of relationship with the selection of objects, if what is constructed there is what we call "universality" (extrapolating it from a narrow, western community), a nagging question remains: Would 10 Corso Como be, in its own manner, the new, mutated version of these ten or so universal museums that western civilization has on record? A priori, the question might seem enigmatic, and yet there are indications that tend to support such a view. First, there is just this presence of different worlds, all conjoined here. Thus we might also identify here a universal museum of contemporary creativity—a place in which all the arts of living and thinking are brought together. Besides, one finds here, as in the universal museum, an equalization of all components that is notably absent from the Museum of Modern Art, where reception must be governed by an effect of immediate rapture in front of works of art with abstract forms of representation—what goes by the name of the "wow" effect.

At 10 Corso Como there is no "wow effect," and (symbolic) figuration is omnipresent: the humanism of the place owes to the fact that everything in it is created by and for the human being. This humanity holds together manifestations of human creativity that hierarchies would otherwise tend to disjoin and separate: cooking, literature, design, art, clothing, souvenirs. Everything has its place there because everything emanates from this great human talent. And one cannot help thinking that here, in this non-hierarchical relation with things, is an element that comes very close to the universal museum, where the thing itself—not the idea of it or the assumptions we make about it—holds it together; where value is inherent and not attributed; where belief occupies less space than its inscription (which is often immediate) in systems of axiological appreciation.

Nevertheless, 10 Corso Como is even closer to the contemporary museum than it is to the universal museum. One cannot help thinking that, two years before the opening of the Milanese institution, Tom Krens became director of the Guggenheim in New York, where he was preparing the definition of what would soon become the embodiment of the contemporary museum. There is a stunning chronological coincidence here; and the parallels between the Guggenheim under Tom Krens' conception and 10 Corso Como as defined by Carla Sozzani are numerous and striking.

In the first place, they both envisage the world starting from the contemporary: the universal museum arises from the depths of the ages it deposits in order to transmit them to us, whereas the contemporary museum captures in the past whatever it wishes and takes hold of it. Thus Carla Sozzani has come to programme, among her exhibitions of contemporary photography, a Horst or a May Ray retrospective, or an exhibition of futurist photography curated by the art historian Giovanni Lista. These moments of the past shed light on the present and justify themselves, at the moment they are shown, as a counterpoint or as a reinforcement. Their relation with history is thus, permanently, an input from the contemporary. Another point of comparison with the Guggenheim is the understanding of the place and of its diffusion. The institution must be firmly anchored in a site that defines it: the Frank Lloyd Wright building on Fifth Avenue, or this extraordinary installation of Carla Sozzani and Kris Ruhs that is 10 Corso Como. And, at the same time, it must spread from this specific anchoring, symbolic and visual. This is why, beginning with the Peggy Guggenheim Collection in Venice, Tom Krens launched projects in Bilbao, Abu Dhabi, Guadalajara, Rio de Janeiro, and Tokyo too, and 10 Corso Como collaborated with Comme des Garçons and many others at the same time. This was hardly an obstacle, if only by reason of the identity of 10 Corso Como. The most visible local anchoring does not diminish diffusion—on the contrary, it facilitates it; for it allow us to make variations starting from a point of identity and to change the lights cast in different places upon the same institution. Today 10 Corso Como exists in Milan as well as in Seoul, Beijing, and Shanghai, and it was in Tokyo for a decade.

What we see here, of course, is the result of

Carla Sozzani's passion for Asia and, more specifically, for China, which she crossed by train in 1980. What we also see—and perhaps especially that—is her understanding of how anchoring enables expansion. Identical in all these places, the name 10 Corso Como bears a very precise meaning in Milan, because it is a local address. On the other hand, in Seoul, Beijing, Shanghai, and New York it exists only insofar as the institution in that location has succeeded in establishing itself above and beyond an address, by containing a world that constitutes an object of desire. The same is true for the Guggenheim: wishing to have a Guggenheim in every corner of the globe has little to do with Solomon R. Guggenheim, the initial donor, or with his history, with the reasons that governed his decision to create a museum, or even with the adventure of the construction of the building itself. At stake here is an identity— some would call it "a brand"—but especially a "methodology," a way of addressing the world and its things.

The methodology of the two institutions, developed as it were simultaneously, is the same: to give to every citizen of the world a view of the world. This is what goes by the name "cosmopolitanism" in the aristocratic culture of the nineteenth century (of which 10 Corso Como is an inheritor) and by the name "global culture" in the open-ended version that the Guggenheim developed. The central idea is simple: what is presented targets citizens of the contemporary world, who belong to an extended, albeit somewhat diluted western culture, but who also pay heed to the distinctive features of every setting where they become established, which come to revitalize somewhat. To this extent, the critics of the Guggenheim have been able to see in it a kind of Trojan horse of the end of the West, which established its narratives, in a last attempt to maintain some kind of validity and power. Tom Krens, its author, regards this tension, much to the contrary, as a will to initiate a constructive relation, a real conversation designed both to keep the West alive and to bring to nations deprived of a museum culture the know-how that the Guggenheim had mastered. Well, this tension can be read at the core of 10 Corso Como's founding model: in fact the point of origin is clearly western—an address in a neighborhood of Milan; and what is represented, both in terms of display and in terms of publications or fashion choice, is essentially western too—it comes from this West that has just changed under the description of "global." Today restaurants all feature Italian cuisine—in Milan, in Shanghai, in Beijing, in Seoul, and in New York.

And it is within this "global" horizon that inspirations from all corners of the globe are integrated, yet kept in due proportion, as if in order to perpetuate the central, western model: this is why Kris Ruhs can be emblematic of the positioning of the Milanese institution. He is a New Yorker of German origin who lives in Milan and speaks French in equal measure: from either side of the Atlantic it would be difficult to envisage a more western identity than his. Nevertheless, it is a whole imagery of the entire world that transpires in the universe of forms he works in, those anthropomorphic images in hanging gardens: the human figures call to mind the totems of primitive art, while the garden can take you to the East—the Near East with the dream of Babylon, the Far East with Japan and China, which embody the art of the garden. And yet everything is integrated in the figure of the artist: a demiurgic, world-creating figure that manifests itself in all the forms, without exception.

In this way 10 Corso Como seems to belong to global culture even more than the Guggenheim. Once in a while the Guggenheim made incursions into this arena, where the motorcycle can be a subject, perhaps of art and certainly of discourse, or where Giorgio Armani deserves an exhibition in the museum; but, as a general rule, it remained faithful to its mission to be a temple of modern art—a mission defined by its collection. 10 Corso Como operates in conformity with a museological way of thinking, but without a collection, and hence without that anchor in modernism by which the Guggenheim defined itself and its mission. Thus, according to a number of principles that seem somehow to command what is being put on display, it can fully embrace this classical postmodernity of global culture.

First of all, what is on display is made: workmanship and fabrication are paramount. 10 Corso Como is not about a marvelous idea realized in a few seconds. Time, the way of doing things, the precision, and the work are integral components. Next, what is on display is taken from a situation to which it fully belongs, displaced as it is and replaced on another horizon: just the fact that it has been made and that its workmanship holds it together allows this exit and displacement. Finally, we are dealing with an object that has a deviant relationship with the present, an object that is not merely inscribed in the unconscious pursuit of its course but ether dramatizes this pursuit or else departs from it radically. At all events it strikes a chord with the consciousness of time, in the contemporary moment itself.

Hence fashion is in some way the backbone of this great body of 10 Corso Como: it is, by virtue of necessity, the medium most immediately conscious of time. It can choose to forget it and to get lost in it—to continue, season after season, to take up whatever there is, and to perpetuate itself without end. Or, as in the case of 10 Corso Como—and this is where the institution's museological signature shows up—fashion can choose to reverse time and wear it like a jacket, both inside and out, in order to show the couture and thereby give food for thought. That is where Carla Sozzani's fashion decisions originate. Craft, and only craft, is what makes a couture recognizable; coutures have to be well made before they can be seen. They can be rendered visible through sheer will of affirmation, once they have been designed and crafted with care—as they are by Rei Kawakubo or Vivienne Westwood, whom Carla Sozzani greatly admires; or they can be rendered visible in the perfection of a form, as in the work of Azzedine Alaïa. These three figures, together with Pierre Cardin, to whom she dedicated two exhibitions at the Galleria, came together just as a result of the crisis they imposed on the accelerated, unconscious passage of time, which is the very oblivion of our contemporary society.

This is also why 10 Corso Como is a museological space: there can be no museum without time specific to the museum. To be sure, it is increasingly common to witness visitors going through museums as if they were ambling through department stores. And it is true that 10 Corso Como is a department store (the department store [*magasin*] being the twin of the magazine [*magazine*]) that we must enter as if we were getting into a museum, or even into a church whose place it has taken. This is a space where, at the heart of the contemporary, at the heart of its things, a deviation has opened that allows the current time to be mirrored and reflected upon, and thus generates the possibility of an inner life.

The subtlety of the place consists, then, in its veering between permanence and impermanence: in appearance, the place does not change. Since the overall impression is always the same, it would be possible to draw an immediate conclusion to the effect that it is definitely a museum. The museum is what never changes—what we have established must not change, according to the model of the universal museum. Yet everything changes all the time, and surreptitiously at that: some books disappear, being replaced by others; clothing styles change every season; and, in reality, one is never in the same place. The contemporary is not, then, the negation of the time that passes, according to the model developed at the Guggenheim and to 10 Corso Como's idiosyncratic style: it is neither a refusal of it nor really its acceleration. It plays its game in an ambiguous, duplicitous space where at one and the same time everything changes incessantly and things remain what they are. The contemporary—such as it is, once it has been museified in this manner—is a deviation inherent in time.

One of the questions that the museum had

to deal with right from the start of its development in the eighteenth century concerns its relation with the public sphere: at once with public space—its access—and with the public as a political notion—its paying heed to the community. For this reason it was in England that the first system of museums was inaugurated—the Ashmolean in Oxford and the British Museum in London. These institutions are free and are often associated with mechanisms of representation and of knowledge that are alien to the pure imperative of aesthetic contemplation: for the Ashmolean, knowledge tied to the university; for the British Museum, an openly English identity. This is an important point because it marks a difference from the art gallery, from the boutique, and even from the art center: none of these three models has it as an a priori calling to be open to the public space and to take hold of the public process so as to absorb it and to become its reflection.

The gallery and the boutique have their own public, on which they count for their sales; the art center has its own public, which comes to consume. But the museum seeks to confront the public, understood in the broadest sense: the child who knows nothing but feels everything, the specialist who knows everything but feels nothing any more; the metropolitan citizen; the visitor from the most faraway places. We find at 10 Corso Como this care for the "public" in the broadest sense: the Milanese setting is not simply about welcoming "a" public that is supposed to purchase everything on display—a specialized public, that of fashion, of design, or of art, indeed even of literature or gastronomy. 10 Corso Como mixes the various publics and, in doing so, creates a total public: one that attempts, all at once, to see beauty, to live in its clothes, and to have exquisite sensory and human experiences. The visitor is not a client: if he or she buys something, so much the better; but that's not the aim. The visitor comes to a museum that is also a public place. Within it lectures, presentations, conversations, events are organized—even a complete reading of the *Divine Comedy*, in 2015. More than just to "consume," the public comes to participate in the act of art in all of its distinct forms: the act of this art that happens to be aesthetic life.

Without saying it in so many words, 10 Corso Como is an arena of combat for our subjectivity: in fact it touches on our relation with the world in a most penetrating manner, as a museum can do. A museum, if it is fully felt and lived, is the most unsettling and most reassuring place in the world: we see everything of perfection and beauty that has been made before our time; we feel the effects of human destruction; we delimit our knowledge and discover, just like the infinite clouds that stretch below us when we fly in a plane, at what point our knowledge is limited. Knowing all that allows us to live better, that is, to live in awareness of our exact place in the world. It is a modest place but a real one, which can be up to the task of conquering the world, once its humbleness is accepted, even flaunted. With the museum we also sense what we have lost of our relation with things: we try to catch with our fingers the digital cloud over which a part of our lives has tipped and, just for an instant and only in this place, it seems possible to retain it.

To the contemporary mind, 10 Corso Como gives the same impression: we feel rightaway the immensity of human creativity. Books, images, objects, clothing, drawings—everything can be found in it, everything is beautiful even when it's the object of a game, everything lies before us. We can realize Brâncuşi's imperative: everything—or almost everything—can be touched. We can run the fabrics through our fingers, caress the design pieces, leaf through the books. What is offered has no hierarchy, and yet everything goes beyond us and leads us into another space.

To be even more precise, through what it excludes, the place gives us an even more intense impression about the point of the selection. With a few exceptions, neither ancient nor "contemporary" art is to be found there. Ancient art is preserved in museums that are disconnected from the world; and "contemporary" art can seem even more disconnected. For its part, 10 Corso Como is clearly in this world of ours: it is a museum in which all the things that multiply around us outside are brought together in an inside. This inside is at once a world of its own and in perfect osmosis with the world: one finds the external things, yet all are transformed through their inclusion. This is really a world at the heart of our world, and one that reflects and magnifies it.

It's a place where we find things, where we look at things and we look at ourselves; a place where the community is invited to perceive, and at the same time each individual has a place; where from time to time the person and the totality that we are find things to converse about.

From its beginning, the Galleria Carla Sozzani has reserved a central place for photography in its programming; this was not the case with painting and sculpture, which were almost absent. This absence carries a piece of evidence: the dream that this place represents has a strong streak of humanist inspiration. Painting very much intensifies our perception of the world; but, in order to have beauty, it must also come from the gesture of a master. To be a great photographer is no small achievement—and Carla Sozzani has shown how much this art we call photography can have diversity and yet submit to its own rules. The mechanism at work is plain to see: painting and sculpture, old elitist and "sublime" forms that have spread everywhere, don't have a place; by contrast, photography, a democratic form whose transcendence is perilous, is marvelously visible. Beyond the simple reality of Carla Sozzani's own human and aesthetic knowledge, which is a consequence of her former editorial work, the fact remains that she has an ambition and a mission: Corso Como is rooted in contemporary democratic humanity, which it elevates through a gesture that is at once firm and delicate. Even in the 1990s, when photography was confined to magazines and books, she had been introduced to it. The proof is in the example she gives that yes, a photograph can be sublime, that it is not only a funerary art, as Roland Barthes used to say, that it is also the possible affirmation of an intensified life—our own.

For this reason one can never let the person out of sight, and the place remains a laboratory for our transcendent experiences: the problem of crowds entering 10 Corso Como does not arise and, if groups of tourists decide to come, it's by their own volition. When the Carla Sozzani Editore team publishes books, these are always magnificent, collector's books, fashioned so as to emanate a feeling of beauty. When an exhibition is presented, it always elicits contemplation from the individual. The garment, which comes conspicuously from the world of couture, is tailored first of all to the individual. The person does not deny the human community but constitutes it.

10 Corso Como is a museum; 10 Corso Como is a forum. This institutional character of the place is especially striking, for it invites asking about the status of its founder, Carla Sozzani. This is

a status that she has invented all by herself, for herself—the person par excellence. When situations demand that she define her goal in setting up 10 Corso Como, this great Italian lady says, very simply: "I wanted to create a magazine that one can touch." As a result, the first identifier that springs to mind is the editor-in-chief that she once was. Certain persons who, like Claudio dell'Olio, continue to work with her today began at the time when she directed *Vogue*. It is easy to see, especially given the eminent role that photography plays in the programming, how there can be a parallelism with the magazine in the way the store operates.

One could even say that that the contribution of 10 Corso Como is to have conceived of a transferable museum of things that are in a photographic state—a museum where things are images and take part in an image. Carla Sozzani would then play the role of the contemporary curator as much as that of a museum registrar who gets attached to objects and keeps them as if they were his or her own forever. For curating makes objects float, disappear, and fade as they are taken in a vertiginous spiral of lists, compositions, and movement.

The history of 10 Corso Como from the 1990s to the present is also that of the rise of the curator—in Italy, the passing of the torch from Germano Celant, who was described as a curator but considered himself a critic, to Massimiliano Gioni, who is truly a curator. It is also a history of working to raise public awareness, a task to which Hans Ulrich Obrist, author of *A Brief History of Curating*[6] and of *Ways of Curating*,[7] has tirelessly devoted himself.

10 Corso Como is the result of a conception of curating in which things assume their existence in our floating, mercurial world; even before the term became a big topic in contemporary debates on our civilization, the Milanese institution had thematized and accelerated the reality it denotes. Curation is a response to the fact that, with the support of photography, from this point on things have become images in the first place.

And yet this primacy of photography does not account for the reality of Corso Como itself; for, from the moment we can touch the objects, they are exposed, they are presented to us, and the job is no longer the same. Another possibility opens, then: Carla Sozzani would have continued in her role as editor-in-chief and would have become an exhibition commissioner. And indeed she organized many exhibitions at 10 Corso Como in twenty-five years—well over a hundred. The place itself is a permanent exhibition that she puts up without cease, a presentation of objects and images in unremitting movement. There as well as in her characterization as "editor," the term is insufficient. For the organization of an exhibition is an isolated occurrence, whereas what Carla Sozzani has created is more in the nature of a kaleidoscopic portrait or programming.

She is ceaselessly programming a view of civilization via the place itself and via the Galleria. Programming in a public space means directing an exhibition center; and, with a project and a vision such as Corso Como embodies, it means in fact having a museum activity. Carla Sozzani is the founder and director of a new kind of museum. She says it herself: "What I do I do for the public, for visitors, for the people who come, hear the birds, and feel the peace. If your goal, your only goal, is to make money, this is not how you do it" [personal conversation]. There is pragmatism and idealism in her approach, both of them remarkable and concomitant. She does not deny that 10 Corso Como generates revenue—after all, the place has to maintain itself—but that is not the goal. Thus on the one hand she does not deny the commercial character of her institution, but on the other hand she absorbs this character into a far wider approach, which belongs precisely to this public mission of Milan, this civilizing mission that Carla has defined for herself and for her project.

The project can be summed up in Dostoevsky's famous and enigmatic assertion that beauty will save the world. The beauty of this world of the ancients, transferred into the universe of global civilization, is that of a contemporary form of the museum. It reintegrates all the values that museums share across the board: the integration of what is rare and what is common, the qualification of an interest in civilization—all these fragments are signs of something about the world they emanate from.

We find there, above all, the great value on which the aristocratic museums of the past were based, a value present nowadays and in this case at the heart of contemporary civilization: connoisseurship. This old value, which is also the supreme virtue of the inborn scholar, that of Bernard Berenson and of Roberto Longhi, is acquired only through incessant work, by exercising a gaze sharpened by looking again and again. Carla Sozzani has never stopped looking at clothes and images; above all, she has never stopped looking at works of ancient art. This world of Italian art—the world of Piero della Francesca and of Carravaggio, two artists to whom she is especially drawn, both of them so conspicuously human, one in the spirit, the other in the flesh—constitutes the horizon within which her thought has been built. She can perceive, and she can think as she perceives: that is what connoisseurship is. She has taken up its practice and ideology to extend its application to a domain where we would never have expected connoisseurship to extend: fashion, photography, and especially the flux of imagery and of image things in our contemporary civilization.

Carla Sozzani herself believes in the museum more than in anything else: she visits museums, thinks about them incessantly. However, as she enjoys the freedom of being the head of her own museum, she can do with it whatever she wants—provided that the public finds here its own place and the aesthetic experience it came looking for. Whether large or small, a museum can be considered an immobile institution that cannot be made to experience anything and will not be able to make us live anything: this is what happens when we shut ourselves within its walls. With Corso Como, the walls have opened and a new model asserts itself.

Museum institutions that define their own identities are not given thematic names thematically. They are most often baptized after their location, be it wide or narrow. The British Museum is in Great Britain; the Metropolitan Museum of Art is in New York; the Hermitage Museum is in the Winter Palace nicknamed Hermitage; the Uffizi is in the Uffizi Palace; the Quai Branly Museum is on the Quai Branly. From the beginning, just by virtue of its name, 10 Corso Como has construed itself as an alternative model of museum; and this alternative model—a few photos here, some clothes there, in a windowless room with a concrete floor—has evolved to become the embodiment of all the questions that arise in the contemporary museum, a place that, more than many others, picks up and adopts our doubts, our desires, and our dreams.

Whether or not this is the result of a will, 10 Corso Como offers us the best possible avenue of inquiry into questions pertaining to the museum. And yet it is not a museum in the institutional sense of the term; it's a model *sui generis*. After all, it sells objects and visitors can leave with what pleases them, be it for a few Euros or a few thousand. Anything is possible. Sure, museum stores have spread everywhere, they are now a proper architectural genre; but it's from the store that one can take an object, not from the museum itself. Besides, the variation in price is not so great in the areas of diffusion of "private products" of the museum.

10 Corso Como's peculiarity is its sales. Thus, if it doesn't enrich its owners, at the very least it allows the place (which does not receive a public subsidy) to survive on its own. At the same time it is not a foundation—because sales transactions take place there. Hence it is a space with a hybrid identity, where everything should in permanence disappear, according to shopkeeping needs. After all, if everything were to disappear, if everything were sold, the commercial success would be total. What would happen if the space were empty? The answer is simple: it would be a space available for meditation. Just as Tom Krens' team had estimated how many visitors

the Guggenheim would attract if it were emptied of its collections—somewhere between 200 and 300,000—we might imagine visitors going to a 10 Corso Como that would be only its own object, as it were. But then it would no longer be 10 Corso Como itself but rather its cenotaph, reminding us that there had been life, things, "collections"—both in the museological sense and as we understand it in fashion—but that, by losing them, the place abandoned a part of its existence.

In the same way, if the contents of 10 Corso Como were entirely removed from the buildings, in Milan and elsewhere, that reproduce its identity, then the very identity of the place would be partially lost; for it is this museum space that things are incrusted, as a permanent repository in a perpetually changing world. A maxim for our time, Lampedusa's remark, "everything has to change so that everything can stay the same," allows us to grasp, with its help alone, the movement embodied in this place. In reality, everything changes: objects, books, images; everything is on display and everything varies; and despite this change, or maybe by virtue of it, everything continues. After all, the museum collections on display in this space are not required to belong to it. This is an infinite and infinitely seductive collection of things waiting to bring us happiness if we are prepared to enter into their fairyland. It is not by chance that Maurizio Cattelan was one of the first to frequent 10 Corso Como from its beginnings; Cattelan's art is based on the transformation of images into things and on the successful transfiguration of a mental image—a shocking and moving *cosa mentale*—into sculpture; all of his creations operate by means of a systematic materialization of images, by a "thingification" of imaginary abstraction. 10 Corso Como proposes the exact opposite: an association of things so that they become a mental image.

This is how a path opens, maybe, for a new model of the museum, one that would take over a part of the fundamental functions of the institution—its mission of public service, its enrolment in public space, its selection of the most remarkable things—but would leave out the limitations inherent in the "museum genre": a tactile model, which grasps things by seeing them and then lets go of them, so that they may in fact remain as they are; a place of transcendence, but of a transcendence whose origin and major justification are among things and in the way we negotiate our lives amid them. Much like in the contemplation of works, and beyond that "wow" of admiration on which modern art is founded, 10 Corso Como—a museum of impermanence, a museum that passes—leads to a humanism where we contemplate what is made by and for us; and it can intensify the reality of our voyage in the world. The institution navigates this ambiguous space in which perhaps we can acquire things— or perhaps not—but where, more importantly, the question does not arise. 10 Corso Como takes us to a seemingly provocative suggestion, but one that occurred to Tom Krens as well: if the works of art are protected, is the museum, by nature, the space where they must be conserved? Or is that not rather this public space built around human beings, where the works can be made visible to everyone from now on—for free in the case of 10 Corso Como, just as it is in English museums?

There would then be two distinct expressions of the museum. One would be the great museum of the world, in which all collections are preserved and accumulate; this great, indeed this divine museum already exists without our being aware of it; it holds together everything that exists. The other would be the museum of presentation, where everyone can live the experience of art, the ecstatic trance that formerly was offered only in churches.

Collecting does not mean simply expressing a judgment of taste. Collecting means allowing judgment to grow beyond its mental or linguistic consistency, letting it spread up to the point of defining the forms of the real, the limits of what has the right to exist and of what does not have a right to survive. By the same token, everything that exists in a culture exists not only by virtue of the act of creation that allowed some object to be born into the world, but also and especially by virtue of the judgment (or series of judgments) that allows every existing object to be chosen by someone, to be part of a collection. Collections are everywhere, and not only in museums or homes. The collection marks the very form of our metropoles; it influences that mysterious physiology of the appearance and circulation of things and forms that we call fashion; it also governs the rhythm of our encounters. But if it is today the force that fashions everything, it is because capitalism has transformed collecting and the collection into the two prime movers of social life. We always forget that purchasing is merely a form in the inflected paradigm of collecting: what is more, in purchasing something we are only moving an object from one collection (the department store) to another (the private home). What we call the market is just the immense sea in which every object and every artifact is supposed to be able to find its collection of choice; the water of this sea is not the desire for profit but the passion for the collection. If this is true, every store and every department store is no more than an ephemeral collection of objects destined to be a basis for the constitution of other collections of objects, and the status of merchandise represents no more than this readiness of an object to move through several collections, to be integrated into anyone's collection. Capitalism has been the extension, to all individuals, of the right to collect—which pertained to an extremely narrow segment of the population; and it has turned the collection into a principle of life and of individuation.

It is this omnipresence of the collection that has turned the museum into a banal space—or rather has turned any space of an object's residence into museal space. From this point of view there is no longer—nor will there be—a *real* distinction between warehouse and museum, or between a gallery and a store. Not only has Carla Sozzani grasped this obvious fact before anyone else, she has built a complete cultural project that is entirely founded on it. In all likelihood, in the memory of our time, Carla Sozzani's name will be associated with that of the concept store and with the toponym that has become synonymous with it everywhere in the world: 10 Corso Como. But we would be wrong to see in this space a simple phase in the blazing evolution that the spaces of sales have undergone since the first revolution wrought by Mary Quant, Barbara Hulanicki, or Vivienne Westwood in London during the 1960s. From a purely formal standpoint, this is much more than a space for sales or a simple boutique. Surely it is also a collection of spaces: a hotel, a gallery, a boutique, a restaurant. But these spaces are not simply juxtaposed, in a relation of spatial contiguity, as they could be in any street in the historical center of an Italian village. This was no longer about multiplying or diversifying people's experiences, adding a sense of contemplation, repose, or restauration to the act of buying. On the contrary, 10 Corso Como constructs a space in which experience has no limits and allows no distinctions. It is about transforming the storehouse into a space of life and total experience, where thing, space, life, society can no longer be distinguished. It is perhaps in this sense that Corso Como represents the most accomplished attempt at transcending the contradictions and oppositions of contemporary avant-gardes and at achieving a total reconciliation of art and life. From the museum to the galleries, contemporary art continues to get mired in mechanisms of exclusion: art is possible only on condition of excluding life, commerce, the everyday, consumption—in other words life itself, in its homogeneous and unitary experience. And it's not by chance that, in order to realize a space simultaneously of exposition and of consumption, Sozzani has preferred to concentrate on the "minor" and "applied" arts, those that have always seemed closest to life: fashion, design, gastronomy, publishing, and especially photography.

In this space photography is more than one object among others. For over twenty-five years 10 Corso Como has been one of the most important spaces for the exhibition of contemporary photography in Italy and in the world at large. And the collection displayed today represents a sort of encrypted journal of it: from Carlo Mollino to Horst P. Horst, from August Sanders to Eberhard Schrammen, from Maso Yamamoto to Robert Polidori: Marcel Duchamp, Nobuyoshi Araki, Urs Lüthi, Duane Michaels, William Klein— almost all the authors included have been the subject of an exhibition in this mythic place. But 10 Corso Como is not simply a place where contemporary photographic research could become visible: photography is its ultimate matrix. Carla Sozzani has often indicated having conceived of this space in an attempt to amplify the pages of her magazine into a three-dimensional space of life, to transform them into walls, shelves, and tables. From a certain point of view this is only a radicalization the visual revolution that Carla Sozzani had the savvy to launch in the pages of *Elle* and *Vogue.* By adding a third dimension, she has made real an experience of which any photography is, through a mysterious agreement, both promise and memory.

The reduction of art to the pure act of creation goes hand in hand with an ancient ambiguity of theological origin. We always believe divinity to be the subject defined by a capacity to create the world; nonetheless, Christian myths explain very clearly that the ultimate cause of God's divinity does not reside in his (or her) capacity to create this world. God is divine especially because he (or she) is the Great Collector: God is the one who, at the right moment, will destroy the world, will bring time to an end by selecting from all those who lived, at all times and in all places, the few dozens of human companions with whom it will be possible to live in eternity. Everything else, not only men and women, but every object, every plant, every animal—the winds, the volcanoes, the clouds, the sky and the earth, the stars, the waters—will disappear. We often forget that it is this act and this power that, more than creation, confer upon God a status of divinity, make God at once an object of terror an object of veneration. The final collection is not only the supreme expression of wisdom and of divine will. It is the finality of every activity, of every event, the real objective of every desire and of every will. Everything conspires toward it, everything exists in order to become a part of it. And yet its status is more than ambiguous. In the act of selecting, of casting aside the great majority of what has existed or of what exists in order to give to an elected few the right to survive or to be resurrected, there is more than a smidgeon of cruelty. The divine mercy that we are told characterizes God the creator, the generosity that had allowed all things to emerge from chaos regardless of their qualities, their merits, or their power, turns topsy-turvy into an unscrupulous ferocity, into the father's Saturnian drive to devour his own children. And yet it's only this act that makes divinity the master (or mistress) of justice. On the other hand, *it is only in the final collection that creation becomes just*: or, better, the final collection *is* the realization, the definitive achievement of the ideal of justice, the gathering of the just. As if justice were a matter of destruction more than of creation or engendering: a destruction of time and of space, before it is an elimination of everything that is not absolutely necessary, urgent, apt to live for eternity. Just a matter of collection.

From this point of view, the originary nature of the photographic act becomes clear. Considered in its metaphysical aspect, any photography is an act of collection: to take a photo means to select a portion of the real, to invest it with light, to choose it by condemning the rest—everything else—to obscurity. More than an act of salvaging the real, the shift of frame is, first and foremost, the supreme exercise of a final optical judgment. Any photograph is an anticipation of the great final collection, an operation that arbitrarily distributes the right to survival and resurrection, the rare place of a paradise of the world's visual memory. And unlike Christian myths, in which the great collector is a wizened sage perfectly aware of what he collects (because he is the one who created it), here the collection is by and large dispersed and arbitrarily shared among a multiplicity of subjects, occasions, and reasons. And it doesn't take place once and for all, but at all times.

As a paradigmatic form of the aesthetic collection, photography is the organ of sentient justice—and this is why it plays a major role in Carla Sozzani's creation, which may seem to be a form of construction of the world in the age of photography. In every photo, the real is summoned to come back to life in the gathering of the elected. In other words, photography is not the mimetic reproduction of the real: rather it is its resurrection. To bring back to life always means making a gift of grace to an object of choice—and especially having to hand enough grace—enough force—to rescue a fragment from overall destruction. The photographer is the person who has this grace to hand, this superhuman sensitivity that allows you to understand what inhabits the world to come, the one that we well always be able to remember. And it is in this act—in its ability to make a collection, in its capacity to cast aside, to select, to consign to oblivion—and not in its capacity to create, that photography has something of the divine. Any art can create and engender, but only photography is capable of choosing, electing, collecting the real. Like gods, photos are not of this world: they come from the world that comes after the end of all things. They are literally a memory that we will have in our future. They are pure images: the exact opposite of memory.

It is, then, in this capacity to produce the Last Judgment all the time that we can understand the intimate, almost consanguineous relationship that ties all of Carla Sozzani's activities—and, more broadly, her cultural, political, and aesthetic projects—to photography. Through photography she has constructed new forms and new grammars for what used to be called "criticism": the activity of judgment, in the will to assemble, one day, the final collection.

3

The Far Ends of Fashion

We spend hours in them every day. And it is within their walls that we find everything that makes our life not only livable but above all beautiful, intense, self-sufficient. Everything we use comes from these places. All the things we love have been nourished by them. All the objects that we can imagine are contained right now, at this very moment, within their walls. The stores are the transcending horizon of every form of objectivity, and yet they seem to be culturally imperceptible.

Unlike what one would think, economy has always neglected these spaces—or, if it has paid them any attention, it has always failed to acknowledge their material, spatial, and symbolic reality. Their necessity is purely instrumental: a store exists insofar as it allows the producer to gain contact with the final consumer—the buyer: it is the phantasmagoria that is vital for masking the imbalance of power and conscience between the two, the detour through spectacle and illusions that is needed for the exchange to take place. Philosophy and the social sciences seem to have followed economy's lack of interest and myopia to the letter. There is nothing either spiritual or symbolic in trade and exchange. They are defined by an operation whose unique goal and unique rationale are the maximization of gain and of utility, an operation in which the symbol can exist solely as lie and deception. In exchange there is no truth other than gain; there is no discourse belonging to commerce or immanent in it that is not the one—brutal, oppressive, deceptive—of the capitalist.

The mistake has been to crush commerce, *negotium,* under exchange, and thus to polarize everything else, everything that is not immediately a condition of possibility required for exchange, into an opposite pole, at once unreal and artificial: the exhibition. As a result, commercial locales become failed or partial museums (because they are limited to the liminal space of the shopwindow) or into dirty museums (since the exhibiting function has been contaminated by purchase—a real *pudendum* to be hidden away, to be ashamed about). By multiplying the spaces for pausing and contemplating that have no links with consumption, by transforming the inside of the commercial site into an immense transit space where one can browse on one's own, 10 Corso Como turns on their head the visible functional hierarchies on which the commercial form is structured. First of all, it assembles and arranges harmoniously, in the same space, the sum of some of the most beautiful things, yet without making them inaccessible or untouchable: the shopwindow becomes a space for pause and living; purchase becomes a way of deepening our encounter with things. The store is not an enclosure for exchange to take place; it is the resonance chamber of things. From this point of view one should look for the origins of 10 Corso Como in the artistic avant-gardes of the 1960s more than in some marketing strategy.

One October, slightly over fifty years ago, any passersby who happened to go through 78th Street in New York would have found themselves in front of a strange spectacle. Having brushed against a wagon built by Richard Artschwager, a tourist would have come across a normal-looking supermarket. But the prices would have stupefied the observer: eggs at $144 to the dozen; pork chops for $49. The elevated prices were not due to an economic crisis but were due to the fact that, in spite of appearances, this was not a supermarket but "a veritable gallery in which the works of a half-dozen eminent pop artists were selling like hotcakes, and in like manner … for a special price one would have offered three for the price of one."[1] Organized by Paul Bianchini, Ben Birillo, and Dorothy Herzka (Roy Lichtenstein's future wife), *American Supermarket* brought together a variety of artists who included Andy Warhol, Robert Watts, Claes Oldenburg, Tom Wesselmann, Jasper Johns, Lichtenstein, and Billy Apple. Mary Inma, a professional artist who specialized in commercial presentations, had prepared replicas of cheeses, meats, and drinks of another genre, but those objects did not claim to be "works of art." The mimetic element in the comparison with traditional spaces devoted to the sale of commodities reached a point where Paul Banchini, the owner of the gallery, was ambling about with a grocer's pad and pencil, to take orders. The exhibition seemed to aim at reproducing Zeuxis' paradox, as described by Pliny the Elder: however, verisimilitude no longer defines the competition between art and nature, but rather that between art and the market, between an artistic object and a piece of merchandise. *American Supermarket* can be thought of as the installation of a three-dimensional still life that tries to call into question the boundaries between gallery and museum. Other artists had attempted and would attempt to work along similar trajectories. In *The Show*, Claes Oldenburg had already assembled, in the same space, all kinds of objects, from clothing to drinking containers, all of similar flesh tone and material, to demonstrate, in his own words, "the unity and non-separation between commerce and art." Allen Ruppersberg's installation *Al's Café* (1969) or Robert Filliou and George Brecht's *La Cédille qui sourit* (*The Smiling Cedilla*), the non-store destined to become a center of permanent creation that was open at Villefranche-sur-Mer between 1965 and 1969, seemed to resonate with quite a few of the features that marked the exhibition in New York. Even so, the radical character of *American*

Supermarket was unprecedented. It was not just a matter of reproducing a decor that resembled a supermarket in order to exhibit an assemblage of pop art; and, unlike in Claes Oldenburg's reproductions of objects of common use, here the goal was not to replace everyday goods with art objects in order to make it possible to reintegrate "the magic proper to the universe," which would allow people to "live in a religious and affable exchange with materials and the objects surrounding them."[2] Nor was it a superficial reproduction of the store form—as in Christo's *Shop Fronts*, which had been on display since the same year—or a deconstruction of the idea of commerce, as in the case of Ruppersberg and Filliou. And there was not a trace of the critical attitude that had informed Paul McCarthy's 2014 exhibition *The Chocolate Factory*, in which the museum—the ancient Paris mint, La Monnaie de Paris—was transformed into a factory of small chocolate statues that represented Santa Claus or plug-like Christmas trees—as if to denounce both the dangerous proximity between money, pleasure, and product and the ambiguity that makes the distinction between them impossible. *American Supermarket* applied a sort of reversal of Duchamp's *readymade*. If the latter introduced a prefabricated object into the gallery in order to change its status and make a work of art out of it, here a series of works of art took on the appearance of goods and everyday objects in order to change the form and the status of the space in which they were *into a genuine store*. The works of art became inseparable from the space of the exhibition, but not because they were inextricably tied to the decor, or because they were site-specific, but because the space itself then seemed to be a pure emanation of the objects present in it. *It is no longer the space (the gallery, the white box) that determines the state of the objects within itself; on the contrary, from now on the objects create and produce the identity of the space.* By transforming the gallery into a "real life store" (Grace Glueck), *American Supermarket* elevated shopping itself to a form of art, making artistic contemplation and life coincide *inside* the market. The store was only the emanation, the effect, the echo of the things that existed inside it. It was in fact the works of art and their sensory appearance that transformed an artistic space into commercial space; and, at the other end, the commercial space itself became a work of art. The store was the object and means of the aesthetic experience par excellence. It was this coincidence between art and the market, between museum and store, that liberated the market from the reality of exchange: the store is only the emanation of the things that are in it.

10 Corso Como is perhaps the heir most aware of this discovery. It is first of all able to radicalize it, to be done with the last remains of the separation, and to realize the identification between art and life for which all the artistic avant-gardes of the beginning of the twentieth century have sought to invent a formula. To construct a store does not mean simply organizing a space in a certain manner: it means putting together things that can transform the space, open it to the power of things.

What is the status of the atmosphere that things create around themselves and that we call commerce? And why is commerce the first effect of the power of things? Conversely, why must things be gathered under the form of commerce in order to exert their own power? In a word, what is the meaning of what we call commerce, if their goal does not express itself in the simple fact of exchange? 10 Corso Como has transformed commerce into the transcendental form of performative reflection on the meaning of things and on their power.

The power of things to give human life a shape and to influence attitudes, thoughts, desires, tendencies, habits, and relations with the world is called style. Style is not something of a purely personal nature; it is not a simple emanation of the character of this or that person. Style is above all a property of things: a painting, a sculpture, a book have style. Sure, this style is considered to be the emanation of the personality that produced this painting, this sculpture, this book; but, through emanation, contiguity, and participation, things can make it so that the style in question becomes the property of hundreds of other men and women. This is the power of any thing whatsoever and not only of those that, for arbitrary reasons, are classified as works of art. Not only paintings or sculpture, but any artifact, of any kind whatsoever, can embody style—and especially can transmit it to anyone who comes near it. And probably this radioactivity of being is exactly what constitutes the ultimate source of our love for things. This radioactivity is what we seek in all things. Because it is the things that we wear, that we don, that we make to adhere to our bodies that allow us to have style. These are the things that we desire and imagine in order to define the shape of our movements. These are the things that we surround ourselves with in order to make the ambient space into a *world*.

10 Corso Como appeared as a Geiger counter, as a detector of the style that inheres in things, as a tireless explorer of the style of things. Before it, this function had been performed by the fashion press—thanks to this revolution of the 1980s that had Carla Sozzani among its great protagonists and that prompted the traditional magazines to open up to the world of style and things without constraints of genre or discipline. Yet, unlike the printed page—which cannot do it unless it restricts itself to this function of representing and scouting—commerce does not limit itself to informing or broadcasting, after the fashion typical to any artistic or cultural history from before 1900, but makes us touch and live things; on the contrary, it makes art into a space of life as well as of contemplation. That is exactly where we find this material radicalization, this spatial veracity of everything that was condemned for a while to be discourse—in liberating the force and power of things. The store becomes then the

place of style or, better, the space in which style is at the same time an attribute of things and one of individuals, passing without interruption between them.

10 Corso Como has changed the store into a place where the medium and the object of aesthetic experience coincide. This is the reason why time in its entirety begins to be characterized by style. Aesthetic experience no longer takes place in time, because it is the primary source of time and of history: what the boutiques have discovered (and what fashion has taught them) is that time is only the echo of an aesthetic experience, not its condition. Memory of the past and apperception of time are no longer tied to the order of things and of events, but to the taste that defines the totality of objects with which they surround themselves. To speak of the 1960s and the 1970s is to name a certain *aesthetic experience, a certain style in the appearance of things and of bodies*, not just a collection of political and social events. We characterize and recognize the periods of the past on the basis of the aesthetic appearance of the things that populated them. Fashion, not history, identifies an era. On the contrary, the world and the era become pure functions of taste and style.

The *concept store* has transformed the relation between aesthetic experience and time, has freed it from the necessity of history. This is also why they are condemned to live outside history, in a topicality different from the present, which can never accumulate and expand into history.

At one point or another, any human existence has to face a heartbreaking situation: we are mortal. No matter what we do, a moment will come when we will no longer be. We can decide to forget it and continue to live; we can take refuge in entertainment; we can equally shut ourselves up in despair; we can believe in an afterlife. For, as the atheist philosopher Quentin Meillassoux has underscored, psychological awareness of the fact that we live on a planet nourished by the flesh of billions of dead people who preceded us makes it unlivable.[3] In order to survive while accepting it, we must envisage the possibility not of a God who is truly a redeemer but of one who raises the dead. In order to live metaphysically we must accept parousia.

Or else we must do the opposite—and accept that the time that remains is the time that builds; like museums or cathedrals, where those who constructed them lived, from which they drew the metaphysical substance of their existence, and which nonetheless survive long after their death, as affirmations of their grandeur—outside the mortal order of the testament. We must accept that life is lived now in order to go on residually after us, and even without us. This acceptance is not possible without courage, without will, and without force.

In the past, deciding to build a cathedral meant knowing that one would never see it completed; and yet one would see it draw toward its completion; one would see the thing, and see it tending toward another existence. Cathedrals were spaces of the awareness of an infinite time. Museums, which came later and have recently multiplied so much, are generally built considerably faster, say, over a decade. They are the monuments of finished and yet extended human time.

10 Corso Como, whose creation follows the age of museums in the Enlightenment, displays the moment of tension in which three apparently antagonistic models come to be in dialogue: the cathedral, where we believe in God; the museum, where we believe in the human being; the store, where we believe in the object. The store's object is not indebted to God for its capacity to produce

meaning—God is quite remote. It is surely indebted to the human being, to whom it owes its creation; but it is especially indebted to itself, to the coalescence of the senses that it proposes. In reality, it is the human being that is indebted to the object, within the store.

From the moment human beings are indebted to objects, they try to define a space of their own, not to owe too much to an isolated object; thus they introduce variety. And therefore they consume. They try to dissimulate their debt through the reduction of instances of indebtedness. Such is the truth of our globalized society. 10 Corso Como bears its conscience; for it is, after all, a boutique. This Milanese boutique has expanded to Tokyo, then to Shanghai, Seoul, Beijing, and New York. In this sense it has integrated the consumption needs of all these societies, which were opening up to our world; it has mobilized them, thereby taking its place in the order of transitoriness, of Pascalian pastime extended to a lot more people than kings and queens. It is true that at all times something is changing at 10 Corso Como. And there we are indeed in the realm of this "accelerated culture" that Douglas Coupland had diagnosed at the end of the 1980s—this civilization that we cover by plane, from town to town, from continent to continent; this civilization that started at the beginning of 10 Corso Como and has expanded with the gigantic planetary alternative that the Internet opens and covers. But we are also confronted by a radicalization of what happens in museums—where, because of loans, exhibitions, and new acquisitions, everything always changes.

It's not just a store. The twenty-five years of 10 Corso Como's life are also a privileged outpost for observing the evolution that has occurred in the world of fashion in the past few decades. From the 1960s on the boutique became the hub of the production of style. From Mary Quant's Bazaar (which opened in October 1955 on King's Road, Chelsea) to Terence Conran, from the series of Biba stores (beginning with the one that opened in September 1964) and from Yves Saint Laurent's Rive Gauche (which opened in 1966) to Mr. Freedom and to Malcolm McLaren and Vivienne Westwood's very famous Sex—the fashion establishment, sometimes single-branded, became the point of creation and invention of new tendencies and new social styles. These were the spaces that would allow fashion to descend into the street—

to recall Yves Saint Laurent's celebrated remark. As Pierre Cardin would say, fashion should not be about a few hundred people, it should be about the millions that were about to ask for new clothes, new style, new lifestyles. These were the spaces that would create a new alliance between haute couture and prêt-à-porter in all major firms. These were the spaces that would turn the street into the theater of a new dandyism and of a new art of browsing—which, unlike its nineteenth-century counterpart, concerned not a minute and marginal public but large swathes of the middle classes. The boutiques are not marginal spaces but centers of a new form of culture, which speaks through things—objects it makes use of—more than through literary or artistic magazines; and it prefers to construct its own identity through a clothing style more than through a series of beliefs and convictions, or through a specific *Weltanschauung*. With the boutique was also born what will come to be called "subculture": the distinction between different groups in the same society is no longer based on hierarchies of class, but on elements of style.[4] The movements of social imitation and emulation that character-ized the nineteenth century are replaced by those of an antagonistic distinction: a minority that stands against hegemonic mainstream culture. Culture, especially the kind that can express itself through style, becomes the theater of the most radical and most important social changes. It was the physiology of subculture that turned the minority into a majority that had to have the new tendencies and the new styles stand against it. From the 1960s on, boutiques became the heart-beat of this new dynamism—global, capillary—in the production of social and cultural identities. The case of the punk movement, entangled as it was with the history of *Sex*, is only the most spectacular example. This was a revolution whose consequences could hardly be fathomed: it was not just a change in the aspect and composition of the social fabric, it was a radical change in the very idea of social life. Over the passing years this dynamism has become radical and has invested the entire society: today the whole culture is the product of the subcultural mechanism at the basis of the creation of styles and tendencies. Culture is only the visible flow of subcultural invention.

10 Corso Como is at once a reaction and a response to this change and, from a certain standpoint, it represents the necessary evolution

of the boutique. Except for the Fiorucci Stores in Milan and New York, boutiques were exclusively focused on fashion clothes and accessories. By widening the number and nature of the objects displayed and sold, the concept carried to its final conclusion the idea that contemporary culture is above all a material culture that reflects itself in a series of objects of things. Today identity is a matter of style and no longer a matter of class, race, religion, salary, or ideology. But style is not made of purely sartorial elements any more: today it invests the indefinite and unlimited series of human artifacts, any object or thing produced in our days. Which means that all relations with things (and not only the one constructed through dress)—from food to contemplation, from furniture to the fastest consumables—become spaces and instruments for the construction of a personal, cultural, and social style and identity. Conversely, things are no longer functional instruments but expressions of a style, of an identity, of a certain form of culture. To put together, to display, and to sell things is the form of making culture that becomes privileged today.

Yet on the other hand the store concept means not only radicalizing the classical model of the boutique but also transforming it. Traditional boutiques were already spaces conceived for the purpose of producing a total aesthetic experience, beginning with the architectural project for their space—a project that was often associated with great creators. Rive Gauche, opened by Yves Saint Laurent, was thought of as a small museum: from Eduardo Arroyo's portrait of the stylist to Isamu Noguchi's lamps and to the statues Niki de Saint Phalle presented inside the court, everything appeared to have been fashioned so as to make the medium coincide with the object of the aesthetic experience. The store became the metaphysical place whose function was to prove that art can give shape, chisel everyday life down to its minutest details: not only the shape and appearance of clients' anatomical bodies, but also the space of these portable works of art—the clothes of a great fashion house—is itself a work of art. From this point of view, the boutique is a space that has to render the white box impossible, to destroy the distance between object and space. But because it proposed first of all clothes—and first of all clothes that express a given style, a given tendency, a given idea of fashion—the store was fated to become again, in time, a marginal space, a place where tendencies and styles were produced, consumed, and forgotten, all in one breath. The concept store went one step further: the point was no longer to elaborate a certain style and to oppose it to the current hegemonic style, or to become the motor of history in order to allow the mind to shuttle from one style to another. Today 10 Corso Como operates an abstraction: it isolates *style as such*, not as a sum or as an eclectic and confused selection of what the street and the worldly salons propose and accept, but as an absolute requirement. The point is not to adhere to one style or another: the invitation to embrace Alexander McQueen's and Martin Margiela's propensity for crossdressing or Rei Kawakubo's antifashion minimalism, punk or hipster, is replaced by the attempt to delimit style as an eternal fact, no longer tied to time and to the present. The store becomes a kind of Noah's ark of a universal style, in which the most valued artifacts are saved from the tempest of history.

Changes occur in the detail, progressively: the whole remains, something changes, the adventure continues. "Everything has to change if everything is to continue," according to prince Salina's famous aphorism in *The Leopard*, which is so right. But, if we want something to change, the change has to be subtle, mobile, the transformation invisible and silent at the beginning, before it reveals itself, in all the brutal and sometimes rough splendor of the revolution. This is the conscience that animates 10 Corso Como. The Milanese institution thus stands in counterpoint to our time and to the relation we keep with it. This is how we can understand the relation of this place with photography: Carla Sozzani's interest instills duration and structure into photography—otherwise art of the moment, dream of immediacy. This is what she finds in her historical studies on form, in Japanese photography of the nineteenth century, which she collects; among these photographers she admires so much, such as Francesca Woodman; in the broad history of fashion photography, where everything seems alive and nothing is ever a given; and in these photographers she defends, whose careers she has built, whose thoughts she shares—such as Paolo Roversi, a magician who transforms the moment. That is also the source of her passion for sepia photography—which embodies a dream of timelessness, the persistence of a model technologically outdated and therefore all the more right.

She cuts through our accelerated temporality where it accelerates most, to the point of becoming, more than ever, the symbol of the present: fashion. Style has always been the spirit of the age manifesting itself in clothing—this kind of osmosis between the general look of things and people, the zeitgeist, and clothing itself, with its exact rules, its texture, its merciless requirement of technical expertise. What prevails today is, beyond doubt, the zeitgeist, which is a changing and unstable spirit, proclaiming global and permanent revolutions that concern directly only a minority—and yet, by extension, entire nations. The rules of clothing are abandoned; and the general look—what one sees in the streets—is totally disconnected from the proposals that the world of fashion puts before our eyes.

10 Corso Como makes use of fashion—the domain of clothing, which is its initial and principal field—to offer the exact counterpoint to what fashion itself has become. The Milanese institution evokes its antiquity through the exhibitions that are associated with the collections on display: therein is a great history of the image of fashion and of its creators themselves, from Horst to Cardin. At the same time, since its very

beginning, it has given special support to the adventure of those who represented, in the world of clothing, a current opposed to this uninterrupted acceleration that dominates the fashion world: Azzedine Alaïa, a couturier who firmly opposed "trends," preferring to study the changes in the woman's body and to propose answers that seemed to her most in tune with the body's own movements—a high or low placement of the waistline, bodily measurements, an opening to all bodies, no matter what they are like; and also the imposition of a prêt-à-porter that was as beautiful, neat, and precise as couture. He proposed a vision of clothing in which the futilities of the event give way to the arrival of a more lasting time, and hence a time whose manifestation matters more than anything that will vanish in a hurry.

Rei Kawakubo from Comme les Garçons and Yohji Yamamoto, whose monograph she brought to fruition: for Rei Kawakubo, deconstruction of clothing, destructuration of its imposed order for the sake of entering, with him, into an ever more radical logic of clothing lines—which, filled with awareness of style, position themselves facing another order, that of carried sculpture [*sculpture portée*], as if it were a manifestation of alterity; for Yohji Yamamoto, permanent tension between the maintenance of an order of couture and the establishment of creative disorder. Martin Margiela, whom Carla Sozzani was one of the first to feature: reuse of rejected clothes and their transformation into couture, an updating of the margins, which are improved.

Each one of these is a break from the falsely assertive temporality of the system of fashion: from archeology to antagonism, to the independent path of tendencies, these are positionings outside the system itself, yet they remain at its core, because 10 Corso Como—by itself and through all the revivals it has given rise to throughout the world, from Los Angeles and New York to Paris and London, let alone all these multibrands transformed into living places—has contributed to the history of the system of fashion, as the latter has constructed itself over the past thirty years.

The great force of 10 Corso Como, of the relationship it has with the contemporary world, derives from being permanently set at an angle, of using as its principles the axioms of counterpoint—archeology, antagonism, ataraxy—and, at the same time, of never refusing the new and revisited brands, which might seem detached from their original horizon, of integrating even Moschino's irony and the postmodernism of Vêtements. The aim is not to position oneself *contra mundum*, to refuse the world as it is; rather it is to integrate it, to keep it close at heart, putting at its core even the tensions that generate its density. Many brands make up 10 Corso Como: brands of clothing, books, the presence of artists, exhibitions, all are part of this densified and intense present that is on offer there—a transitory present, but one in dialogue with the feeling of the eternal.

Intensity could be described as a "modern sickness"—the fascination of our civilization with the intensification of an existence considered insufficiently spirited in itself. We used to do everything we could to intensify our existence so as to live in the present. 10 Corso Como represents an extremely elaborate system of intensification; yet its intensification is neither loud nor violent. It is an intensification through peace, which places everything in the horizon of what counts for the great values of beauty and harmony.

These are, of course, classical, aristocratic values; and one cannot help thinking that Carla

Sozzani, who has imposed them on two of the world's continents, between Asia and America, is from Mantova and has grown up in this city, which hosts one of the most perfect examples of harmonious accomplishment in art: she has seen, as a child, Mantegna's Camera degli sposi (Bridal Chamber); she has seen his perfect figures of courtiers dancing with one another. And it was this universe that she has sought to perpetuate: a human universe that ensures that through Gandhara, the Buddhas and the Apollos can look like each other.

Whoever walks into 10 Corso Como will have a strange sense of eternity, of something that goes beyond the limits of an era. No doubt, if the Eternal were to enter 10 Corso Como, it would feel to what extent things are transitory. 10 Corso Como is, for our time, an equivalent of what the Buddhas of Gandhara represented for civilizations: a space in which two different spaces, hence in tension, meet and unite. In this space the two orders are porous vis-à-vis each other and hence can communicate, so that at any point in time you find there the two perceptible realities, depending on what you are looking for: the eternal and the absolutely transitory.

This order of time exists in us, and it also exists outside us. This is how we can understand its presence within the garden. 10 Corso Como is a *hortus conclusus*, an enclosed garden where miracles take place—on this account it is separated from the world and battles with nature; but by force of being *conclusus*, the garden is one of a domesticated nature, of a nature that is already human; the humanity that found its theater at 10 Corso Como aims quite rightly at a dream of nature. If the place is a *hortus conclusus,* at the same time it represents a *domus aperta* [open house]. The hanging gardens that appear intermittently are a sign of this tendency. Fashioned from human materials by human hands, they nonetheless reproduce the face of nature, and they succeed in creating an even more magical illusion of it than is the nature now gone from our cities. This double movement is permanent in these places.

The importance of 10 Corso Como within the history of fashion, and even within fashion industry history, is well known. It is enough to recall that, as is often remarked, it was with reference to 10 Corso Como that the expression "concept store" was used for the first time—an expression about to be used ad libitum soon after, in a plethora of press reviews and articles. In this phrase the term "concept" is often understood in a journalistic sense. A "concept" would be a form of advertising presentation that unites different things under the umbrella of a single approach. In this capacity, the concept would be nothing but a gaze—that of the curator, the director of transitory museum, in other words Carla Sozzani. There would be, then, a contradiction in terms, since the principle of a concept, as it is defined in philosophy in the aftermath of Plato's *eidos* [form], is exactly the reverse of the gaze: it is the intangible and supreme reality that the gaze is attempting to embrace, albeit never succeeding more than in part.

There are grounds for taking this expression seriously and for realizing that what definitely transpires in all the things on display in 10 Corso Como has to do with this sublime horizon of the *eidos* even more than with the concept itself. *Eidos* is what the mind captures in a moment of ecstasy, what Malraux had once called the "absolute" captured in a moment of "elusiveness." The force of 10 Corso Como is to capture the soul exactly when it is ready to abandon itself to consumption—to this frenzy of a jolly distraction, which is also the dissolution of its hope—and to launch it toward meditation and peace. Such is the use of this total installation, the place itself, which reproduces itself in this way from city to city.

We can also discern the influence that this model has exerted upon another of these institutions of commerce: Dover Street Market, which opened in 2004 at its London address, in the image of its Milanese source of inspiration, and from there replicated itself in Tokyo, in collaboration with 10 Corso Como, in order to open later in New York, Los Angeles, and Singapore. But Dover Street Market is directly associated with the brand from which it emanates, namely Rei Kawakubo's Comme des Garçons. We can also think of Colette, in Paris from 1996 to 2017, who built the structure of the bar, of the store carrying souvenirs, objects, clothing, designs, books, and so on, around a certain vision of the world; and the term itself has spread into metropoles and even into smaller cities, where it can be found today, an English term for a Milanese creation of concept stores. And yet 10 Corso Como is not only the archetype of the concept store but carries this worldview that separates it from multibrands such as Harrod's or Liberty's in London, Bergdorf Goodman and Sacks in New York, the Bon Marché and the Galeries Lafayette in Paris—or formerly Maria Luisa, also in Paris.

The more other concept stores carry in them merely the name of the original "concept"—for their primary aim is disruption, interruption, the iterative crises of taste, which block the path toward transcendence and display the image of an immanence that battles without respite the danger of exhaustion—the more is 10 Corso Como a real boutique of the concept, because it makes the concept manifest and accessible in things—which are only its fragments. This is the reason why, much as from a museum, we can take from 10 Corso Como any number of "derivatives": pens, umbrellas, t-shirts. They are a kind of emanation of the absolute *eidos* [Platonic form] of the museum, which has been given to embrace a moment of time, down here. There is in this, of course, a persistence of the civilization of the derivative product—but this derivative product is not simply a reduction of the aura of images sanctified by profane societies, in an extension of Baudelaire's diagnostic, then

Benjamin's. Every object taken from 10 Corso Como is without image: the letters of the name are visible, together with a few features, but no representation is offered.

The *eidos* displayed there is an *eidos* without a masterpiece, without a strong image; an *eidos* where the form itself of the experience offered there embodies access to the ideal; an *eidos* that allows us to grasp an experience beyond the moment, yet an experience firmly bound to the contemporary in all its forms, provided that they are harmonious.

10 Corso Como is, after all, a political creation —in the sense that it reminds human beings about to give themselves to it what this single fact of living as human beings means. The place is a forum of harmonies assembled in a single sound; these harmonies do not refuse dissonance. Much to the contrary. They make it integrate with itself because, just as the great image has no form, great harmony has no contained perfection. Just as the place is open to all, in all cities where it happens to be, in reality, beyond the objects themselves, it asks for an engagement with existence. It is both the most democratic—open place, free admission—and the most demanding.

At the very moment when politics was building itself as a unified global space—when it became a fragmented space, in which all identities were forced to be in relation with one another from now on, to situate themselves vis-à-vis one another, often even in individuals who brought some together in conflict and did not accept it—at that very moment we tried to forget what constitutes the specific feature of being human: the finitude, the dream of sacredness that possess us, "animals and humans" that we are. 10 Corso Como reminds us of this dream of sacredness, which is ours and dominates its powerful and subtle architecture; it reminds us of it with objects, though them. For at 10 Corso Como we know that objects are just a transient means to go beyond a transitory experience. It is a construction that seems to open for us the happy possibility of a life without us; and this construction is, of course, our own. This construction fascinates us because it recalls the possibility of a human time outside the time of humans—this possibility we had forgotten about, caught as we are in our lives, caught in our rhythms.

This adventure that bears the name of an address makes it so that the address itself becomes, by metonymy, that adventure, the collection, and joins the ranks of the musée du Quai Branly, the Louvre, the Hermitage, and the Uffizi. The form becomes the content. All these buildings and places have become instantiations of the human idea, which had come to deposit itself and instantiate itself there in things. Hence they managed to get out of their immediate locations and become fragments of the universal—because in the entire world these place names have become significant symbols, even beyond the Florentine, Parisian, or Saint-Petersburgian addresses they had in the beginning. 10 Corso Como has reached the beyond of universality; for it dreamt of a world beyond humans, a non-political but essential universal and, as it dreamt of it, it constructed it—fragment by fragment, piece by piece.

It is in constructing a new universal, in perpetually shaping meaning at a new cost that we can finally discover it; there is no conflict between construction and discovery, as was often believed, naively. In reality they are the two facets of the same activity: that it is given to human beings, momentarily conscious of the sublime tragedy of their lives, to perceive, stepping beyond what had begun, at the start of the 1990s, like a garage opened to clothing and photographic images, only to become the temple of the dream of the eternal—a dream that exists only insofar as it is transitory.

Postface

At Calm

It is late, two o'clock in the morning. The last visitor has just left. Light falls on this place, which remained animated up to that moment. The store is closed, and so too the library. The restaurant and the bar are still lively. Music is playing, people are moving, words could be heard until then through the fountain and the abstractions of forms across civilizations. Italian is audible, but also English, Japanese, Spanish, French, and other idioms as well.

They have all left. The serpentine entrance is now closed, but only for a few hours. If, then, one is alone in these places, one can live in the empire of things: articles of clothing, which are there, unlit but only touchable, photographs barely visible in the shadows of the night, books that can't be read, foods not yet prepared, cocktails still unmixed: the totality of this integral civilization, which is assembled here without humans, but owing them everything. In a strict sense, nothing is natural here, and yet everything has become second nature, fully human and fully autonomous, functioning according to its own norms.

The museum makes us think that it needs no one; and yet, like Hubert Robert's Louvre, it would quickly disappear if were not looked after every day. We forget its fragility—and that is its genius. At this very moment everything seems to be in place at 10 Corso Como: the places that remain—their parts, chandeliers, murals, fountains—and the objects in them, come and go, all give the impression of being at the same level, all equal in status, and all in time. The truth is that they are not; and yet at this time of the night, when everyone is gone, one could well believe it. The objects could make the absent human feel that they have a life of their own, and that this autonomous life unites them like a parallel city. In the night, things are in the city, neighboring the plants that inhabit these places, just as they neighbor humans throughout the day; they are at calm, they aren't being touched, they exist for themselves.

When the day breaks and the place opens afresh for a curious public, some snatches of this silent conversation the objects hold among themselves will no doubt remain; and it will be possible to believe, for a few seconds, that they can exist without human beings but are there nevertheless for them, when they arrive; and that they are available. This belief is a great achievement for humankind, no doubt one of the greatest: to manage being able to make itself believe, for an instant, that the world exists without it, in a space entirely conceived by it.

In the morning, having come from all over, from around the corner as well as from the other side of the globe, people will, again, encounter all their things, in their diversity and porosity. They will sense their place among them, their propriety, and also the great freedom of things, which finds its origins in them and outside them. And they will be able to leave with them or with a part of them: they can do so—they don't have to do so. But just this possibility indicates that the world is more open, more transactional, and more transitory than it may seem to be in a museum; and yet, there too, it is. 10 Corso Como is the site of the acute conscience of the features of the museum; for it is not one, as it possesses the human distinction—or it is not a museum yet.

Notes

Notes to Chapter 1

1 Plutarch, *Life of Romulus*, 11.2.
2 Pseudo-Longinus, *On the Sublime*, 9.2.
3 C. Barnett Newman, "The Sublime Is Now," *Tiger's Eye*, 1.6 (1948), p. 51.
4 Carolyn Lanchner, in *Constantin Brâncuși* (New York: MOMA, 2010).
5 Carla Sozzani, Interview with Orlole Cullen in "The Sozzani Sisters," in *Italian Style Fashion since 1945: Exhibition Organized by the Victoria and Albert Museum, London*, ed. Sonnet Stanfill (London: V&A Publishing, 2014), p. 263.
6 Dave Hickey, *The Invisible Dragon: Essays on Beauty* (Chicago: University of Chicago Press, 2012).
7 Olivier Zahm, *Une Avant-garde sans avant-garde: Essai sur l'art contemporain* (Dijon: Presses du Réel, 2017), pp. 10–16.

8 Frank Fanselow, "The Bazaar Economy or How Bizarre Is the Bazaar Economy Really?" *Journal of the Royal Anthropological Institute*, 25.2 (1990), pp. 250–65, esp. 262.

9 Ibid., p. 253.

10 Ibid., p. 254.

11 Ibid., pp. 255–6.

12 David Wengrow, "Prehistories of Commodity Branding," *Current Anthropology*, 49.1 (2008), pp. 7–34.

13 Ibid., p. 25

14 Ibid.

15 On the contemporary brand, see Liz Moor's important *Rise of Brands* (London: Berg, 2007).

16 Hardly by chance, the first groundbreaking discussion of value in marketing is B. Gardner and S. Levy's famous article "The Product and the Brand" (*Harvard Business Review*, March–April 1955, pp. 33–9), which lays stress on the impossibility of referring consumer activity to purely social determinants, which the French sociological tradition that runs from Tarde to Bourdieu does persistently.

17 Ibid., p. 35.

18 Ibid.

19 See David Ogilvy, "The Image of the Brand," *Advertising Age*, 26.1 (1955), p. 17.

Notes to Chapter 2

1 Friedrich Naumann, "Werkbund und Handel," in *Jahrbuch des Deutschen Werkbundes*, 1913, p. 13.

2 Friedrich Kiesler, *Contemporary Art Applied to the Store and Its Display* (New York: Brentano's, 1930).

3 Michèle Gazier, *Leila Menchari, la Reine Mage* (Arles: Actes Sud, 2017).

4 See the catalogue *Das grosse Stillleben: The Big Still Life/Le petit Grand-Magasin* (Basel: Reinhardt Friedrich Verlag, 2004).

5 Francesco Morace, "Nuovi luoghi per il consumo Zen," *Interni* magazine, December 1991.

6 Hans Ulrich Obrist, *A Brief History of Curating* (Dijon/Zürich: Presses du Réel/JRP Ringier, 2008).

7 Hans Ulrich Obrist, *Ways of Curating* (New York: FSG, 2014).

Notes to Chapter 3

1 Calvin Tomkins, "Art or Not, It's Food for Thought," *Life* 20 (November 1964), p. 138. On the exposition, see Christoph Gunenberg and Max Hollein, in *Shopping: A Century of Art and Consumer Culture* (Ofildern: Hatje Cantz, 2002).

2 *Store Days: Documents from "The Store" (1961) and Ray Gun Theater (1962)*, selected by Claes Oldenburg and Emmet Williams (New York: Something Else Press, 1967).

3 Quentin Meillassoux, "Dieu à venir, deuil à venir," *Critique*, 704–5 (2006), pp. 105–15.

4 Dick Hebdige, *Subculture: The Meaning of Style* (London: Routledge, 1979).